The Wit and Wisdom of
MARK TWAIN

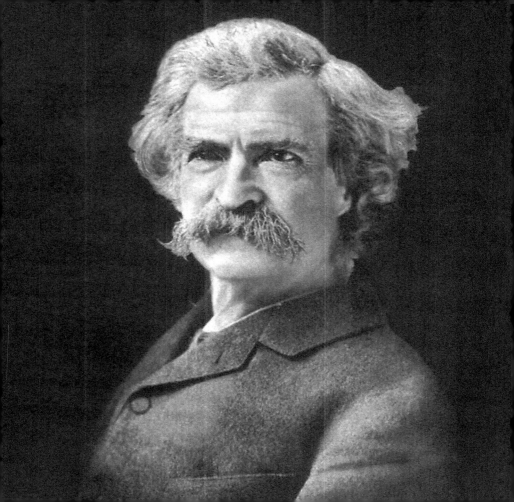

THE WIT AND WISDOM OF

MARK TWAIN

Edited by Bob Blaisdell

DOVER PUBLICATIONS
GARDEN CITY, NEW YORK

Bibliographical Note

The Wit and Wisdom of Mark Twain is a new work, first
published by Dover Publications in 2013.

Library of Congress Cataloging-in-Publication Data

Twain, Mark, 1835–1910.
[Works. Selections]
The wit and wisdom of Mark Twain / Mark Twain ; edited by Bob Blaisdell.
pages cm
A new work with selections from a 25-volume set of Twain's collected
works and from some of the many collections of Twain quotations.
Includes bibliographical references.
ISBN-13: 978-0-486-48923-0 — ISBN-10: 0-486-48923-X
1. Twain, Mark, 1835–1910—Quotations. 2. Quotations,
American. I. Blaisdell, Robert, editor. II. Title.
PS1303.B53 2013
818'.409—dc23
2013000359

Manufactured in the United States of America
48923X07=====2022
www.doverpublications.com

CONTENTS

INTRODUCTORY NOTE

> Wit and Humor—if any difference it is in
> duration—lightning and electric light.
> —*Mark Twain's Notebook* (1935)

We expect Twain's wit but, as with lightning, we can't predict just when and where it's going to strike. His humor, as he says, was electric and seemed to hum along, keeping himself out of the dark until his lightning struck again and illuminated the world.

The boy who was born in 1835 and grew up as Samuel Clemens on the Mississippi River flung himself out into the four corners of the globe, where, as Mark Twain, he became America's most beloved author. In *Tom Sawyer, Detective*, he describes the mysterious force that drew him away from the Mississippi: "It's spring fever. That is what the name of it is. And when you've got it, you want—oh, you don't quite know what it is you *do* want, but it just fairly makes your heart ache, you want it so! It seems to you that mainly what you want is to get away; get away from the same old tedious things you're so used to seeing and so tired of, and see something new. That is the idea; you want to go and be a wanderer; you want to go wandering far away to strange countries where everything is mysterious and wonderful and romantic. And if you can't do that, you'll put up with considerable less; you'll go anywhere you *can* go, just so as to get away, and be thankful of the chance, too." By the time he was 31, he well knew the inner demons that could induce his fever to travel; in a letter to his mother he writes: "You observe that under a cheerful exterior I have got a spirit that is angry with me and gives me freely its contempt. I can get away from that at sea, and be tranquil and satisfied." As an old man, his sense of humor, though dented and punctured, never stopped rolling. His sense of humor kept sparking something inside him and energized him.

No one else in American literature has entertained as many people, and no one before or since has spun the web of his humor so widely, in so many directions. He possessed, as he described it, "the first virtue of a comedian, which is to do humorous things with grave decorum and without seeming to know that they are funny." His progeny are legion, from James Branch Cabell, Langston Hughes, and James Thurber to Garrison Keillor, Calvin Trillin, and Ian Frazier, and all of them as peculiarly American. As Twain explained in "How to Tell a Story": "To string incongruities and absurdities together in a wandering and sometimes purposeless way, and seem innocently unaware that they are absurdities, is the basis of the American art." His art found him a way to write about almost anything, including his bête noire, religion: "I cannot see how a man of any large degree of humorous perception can ever be religious—except he purposely shut the eyes of his mind and keep them shut by force." Our most humorously perceptive American was racially and culturally tolerant, beneficent and generous, scrupulous and guilt-ridden, yes; but religious, no. He insisted we couldn't know ourselves, yet he ruthlessly and sometimes hilariously laid himself bare for himself and us to see.

He was a great reporter who tried not to bore himself and never hesitated to abandon facts for comedy, always his saving grace. He was seriously devoted to his wife and daughters, yet his humor stopped there, at his sole sacred subject, Womankind. He did not dare seriously mock women and so somehow preserved them for himself, either refusing or unable to create them on the page. Women, after all, were rescuing civilization: "we are so stupid that we can't see that we thus plainly admit that no civilization can be perfect until exact equality between man and woman is included." He didn't seem able to appreciate women of artistic mind, famously dismissive of Jane Austen's and George Eliot's novels: "I often want to criticize Jane Austen, but her books madden me so that I can't conceal my frenzy from the reader; and therefore I have to stop every time I begin." Well . . . we all have weaknesses; two or three writers in history have had his strengths. He felt himself a lucky man, for the most part, until one of his daughters died in 1896 and his wife died in 1904.

He was cranky and funny, blue and funny, dark and funny, and delightfully funny. He was so smart he sometimes made us believe he was only funny or underestimate him because he was funny. As Twain's contemporary Leo Tolstoy said of the short story master Anton Chekhov, who underestimated his own powers: "How is it Chekhov can't see that the most priceless part of his art is the humor? A humorist like him is the very rarest of things."[1] Twain was one of those rare things—but he knew the gift humor gave him. When he died in 1910, his death was no longer "greatly exaggerated." A hundred years later, the first volume of his bombshell autobiography made him a bestselling author again. May his renewed and deserved popularity never be extinguished![2]

The quotations I've gathered here come from mining—mining a 25-volume set of Twain's collected works and digging through (an anthologist's phrase meaning *stealing from*) some of the many fine col-

---

1. Tatyana Tolstoy quoted her father in *Tolstoy Remembered* (1978).
2. Twain's Autobiography has had so many versions, even prior to the first official volume of it, that I have noted the dates from the years either Twain or an editor published selections from them.

lections of Twain quotations, most notably Caroline Thomas Harnsberger's *Mark Twain at Your Fingertips: A Book of Quotations* (Dover 2009). Some of his famous sayings . . . he never said, at least not until someone else had said or written them first; some were recalled by acquaintances when he was dead, and Twain then tended to hold his peace even when misquoted. I have included several apocryphal quotations, labeled as "attributed," when their pervasiveness in quotebooks might have made their exclusion here seem accidental (e.g., "Golf is a good walk spoiled"). The subject-categories are simply some of the ones Twain's interests, passions, and obsessions seemed to suggest.

—Bob Blaisdell

Advice and Opinions

Few things are harder to put up with than
the annoyance of a good example.

"Pudd'nhead Wilson's Calendar,"
The Tragedy of Pudd'nhead Wilson (1894)

Nothing so needs reforming as other people's habits.

"Pudd'nhead Wilson's Calendar,"
The Tragedy of Pudd'nhead Wilson (1894)

Always obey your parents, when they are present.
Most parents think they know more than you do;
and you can generally make more by humoring that superstition
than you can by acting on your own better judgment.

Speech, "Advice to Youth" (c. 1882)

You ought never to take anything that don't belong to you—
if you cannot carry it off.

"Advice for Good Little Boys" (1865)

Always do right. This will gratify some people and astonish the rest.

"Note to Young People's Society" (February 16, 1901)

MARK TWAIN

If a person offends you, and you are in doubt as to whether it was intentional or not, do not resort to extreme measures; simply watch your chance and hit him with a brick.

Speech, "Advice to Youth" (c. 1882)

Never tell a lie—except for practice.

Mark Twain, Archibald Henderson (1912)

Don't part with your illusions. When they are gone you may still exist but you have ceased to live.

"Pudd'nhead Wilson's New Calendar," *Following the Equator* (1897)

We all think we are swimming out vigorously on the ocean, while, as a matter of fact, we are each of us paddling around in our own little mud puddle. If you try to get a man out of his private, individual mud puddle he is lost. No man can swim in another man's mud puddle, so when I have a plan that is different from other people's plans they can't understand it, and I have to swim around alone in my own puddle.

Interview, "Mark Twain Talks," *Buffalo Express* (July 30, 1899)

Experience, the only logic sure to convince a diseased
imagination and restore it to rugged health.
The American Claimant (1892)

How can I advise another man wisely, out of such a capital as
a life filled with mistakes? Advise him how to avoid the like?
No—for opportunities to make the same mistakes do not
happen to any two men. Your own experiences may possibly
teach you, but another man's can't. I do not know anything for
a person to do but just peg along, doing the things that offer,
and regretting them the next day. It is my way and everybody's.
Letter (January 16, 1881)

. . . habit is habit, and not to be flung out of the window by any man,
but coaxed downstairs a step at a time.
Personal Recollections of Joan of Arc (1896)

MARK TWAIN

[An Englishman:] A person who does things because they have been done before. [An American:] A person who does things because they haven't been done before.

Mark Twain's Notebooks (1883)

A great and priceless thing is a new interest! How it takes possession of a man! how it clings to him, how it rides him!

A Tramp Abroad (1880)

. . . there is more real pleasure to be gotten out of a malicious act, where your heart is in it, than out of thirty acts of a nobler sort.

Autobiography (July 8, 1908)

If you should rear a duck in the heart of the Sahara, no doubt it would swim if you brought it to the Nile.

The Gilded Age (1873)

You can straighten a worm, but the crook is in him and only waiting.

More Maxims of Mark, Merle Johnson (1927)

We should be careful to get out of an experience only the wisdom that is in it—and stop there; lest we be like the cat that sits down on a hot stove-lid. She will never sit down on a hot stove-lid again—and that is well; but also she will never sit down on a cold one anymore.

"Pudd'nhead Wilson's New Calendar," *Following the Equator* (1897)

He was a good enough sort of cretur, and hadn't no harm in him, and was just a genius, as the papers said, which wasn't his fault. We can't all be sound; we've got to be the way we're made. As near as I can make out, geniuses think they know it all, and so they won't take people's advice, but always go their own way, which makes everybody forsake them and despise them, and that is perfectly natural. If they was humbler, and listened and tried to learn, it would be better for them.

Tom Sawyer Abroad (1894)

A genius is not likely ever to discover himself; neither is he very likely to be discovered by his intimates; in fact I think I may put it in stronger words and say it is impossible that a genius—at least a literary genius—can ever be discovered by his intimates; they are so close to him that he is out of focus to them and they can't get at his proportions; they cannot perceive that there is any considerable difference between his bulk and their own. They can't get a perspective on him, and it is only by a perspective that the difference between him and the rest of their limited circle can be perceived.

Autobiography (May 26, 1907)

The man with a new idea is a crank, until the idea succeeds.

Following the Equator: A Journey Around the World (1897)

A man's brain (intellect) is stored powder;
it cannot touch itself off;
the fire must come from the outside.

Mark Twain's Notebook

A man never reaches that dizzy height of wisdom
when he can no longer be led by the nose.

Mark Twain's Notebook

I would rather have my ignorance than another man's knowledge, because I have so much more of it.

Letter (February 10, 1875)

The older we grow the greater becomes our wonder at how much ignorance one can contain without bursting one's clothes.

Speech, "University Settlement Society" (January 2, 1901)

It was not my opinion; I think there is no sense in forming an opinion when there is no evidence to form it on.
If you build a person without any bones in him he may look fair enough to the eye, but he will be limber and cannot stand up; and I consider that *evidence* is the bones of an opinion.

Personal Recollections of Joan of Arc (1896)

Opinions based upon theory, superstition, and ignorance are not very precious.

Letter (January 27, 1900)

Tom said the trouble with arguments is, they ain't nothing but *theories*, after all, and theories don't prove nothing, they only give you a place to rest on, a spell, when you are tuckered out butting around trying to find out something there ain't no way *to* find out. And he says: "There's another trouble about theories: there's always a hole in them somewheres, sure, if you look close enough."

Tom Sawyer Abroad (1894)

. . . life does not consist mainly—or even largely—of facts and happenings. It consists mainly of the storm of thoughts that is forever blowing through one's head.

Mark Twain's Autobiography (1924)

Every one is a moon, and has a dark side which he never shows to anybody.

"Pudd'nhead Wilson's New Calendar," *Following the Equator* (1897)

ADVICE AND OPINIONS

9

What a wee little part of a person's life are his acts and his words!
His real life is led in his head, and is known to none but himself . . .
Biographies are but the clothes and buttons of the man—
the biography of the man himself cannot be written.

Mark Twain's Autobiography (1924)

There is not one individual—including the reader and myself—
who is not the possessor of dear and cherished unpopular
convictions which common wisdom forbids him to utter.
Sometimes we suppress an opinion for reasons that are a credit
to us, not a discredit, but oftenest we suppress an unpopular
opinion because we cannot afford the bitter cost of putting it forth.
None of us likes to be hated, none of us likes to be shunned.

"The Privilege of the Grave" (September 18, 1905)

I believe that our Heavenly Father invented man because he was
disappointed in the monkey. I believe that whenever a human being,
of even the highest intelligence and culture, delivers an opinion
upon a matter apart from his particular and especial line of interest,
training, and experience, it will always be an opinion of so foolish
and so valueless a sort that it can be depended upon to suggest to our

Heavenly Father that the human being is another disappointment,
and that he is no considerable improvement upon the monkey.

Autobiography (November 24, 1906)

... we do not deal much in facts when we
are contemplating ourselves.

"Does the Race of Man Love a Lord?"

Loyalty to petrified opinion never yet broke
a chain or freed a human soul.

Notebook (1935)

We are nothing but echoes. We have no thoughts of our own,
no opinions of our own, we are but a compost heap made
up of the decayed heredities, moral and physical.

Mark Twain's Notebook

It is not best that we should all think alike;
it is difference of opinion that makes horse races.

The Tragedy of Pudd'nhead Wilson (1894)

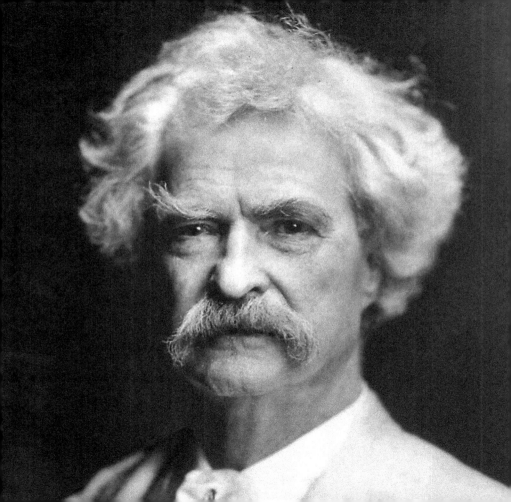

AGES, AGING, AND THE LIFE SPAN

Life is too long and too short.
Too long for the weariness of it;
too short for the work to be done.

Mark Twain, a Biography, Albert Bigelow Paine (1912)

Happy youth, that is ready to pack its valise,
and start for Cathay on an hour's notice.

The Gilded Age (1873)

I was born modest, but it didn't last.

Speech, "Layman's Sermon" (March 4, 1906)

There is no sadder sight than a young pessimist.

Notebook

Life would be infinitely happier if we could only be
born at the age of 80 and gradually approach 18.

Autobiography with Letters, William Lyon Phelps (1939)

When I was a boy in Missouri I was always on the lookout for invitations but they always miscarried and went wandering through the aisles of time; and now they are arriving when I am old and rheumatic and can't travel and must lose my chance.

I have lost a world of delight through this matter of delaying invitations. Fifty years ago I would have gone eagerly across the world to help celebrate anything that might turn up. It would have made no difference to me what it was, so that I was there and allowed a chance to make a noise.

The whole scheme of things is turned wrong end to. Life should begin with age and its privileges and accumulations, and end with youth and its capacity to splendidly enjoy such advantages. As things are now, when in youth a dollar would bring a hundred pleasures, you can't have it. When you are old, you get it and there is nothing worth buying with it then.

It's an epitome of life. The first half of it consists of the capacity to enjoy without the chance; the last half consists of the chance without the capacity.

Letter (July 19, 1901)

The man who is a pessimist before 48 knows too much;
if he is an optimist after it, he knows too little.

Letter (March 14, 1905)

At 50 a man can be an ass without being an optimist
but not an optimist without being an ass.

More Maxims of Mark, Merle Johnson (1927)

It was on the 10th of May—1884—that I confessed to
age by mounting spectacles for the first time, and in the
same hour I renewed my youth, to outward appearances,
by mounting a bicycle for the first time.
The spectacles stayed on.

Speech, "Dinner Speech" (September 1884)

Twenty-four years ago, I was strangely handsome.
The remains of it are still visible through the rifts of time.
I was so handsome that human activities ceased as if spellbound

when I came in view, and even inanimate things stopped to look—
like locomotives, and district messenger boys and so on.
In San Francisco, in the rainy season I was
often mistaken for fair weather.

Letter, unmailed (September 8, 1887)

Experience teaches us only one thing at a time—
and hardly that, in my case.

Letter (February 5, 1893)

I am too lazy, now, in my sere and yellow leaf,
to be willing to work for anything but love.

Letter (January 28, 1882)

The older we grow the greater becomes our wonder at how much
ignorance one can contain without bursting one's clothes.

Speech, "University Settlement Society" (February 2, 1901)

And I wish to urge you this—which I think is wisdom—
that if you find you can't make seventy by any
but an uncomfortable road, don't you go.

Speech, "Seventieth Birthday" (December 5, 1905)

I am old; I recognize it but I don't realize it.
I wonder if a person ever really ceases to feel young—
I mean, for a whole day at a time.

Letter (January 24, 1906)

When I was a boy, there was but one permanent ambition among my
comrades in our village on the west bank of the Mississippi River.
That was, to be a steamboatman. We had transient ambitions of
other sorts, but they were only transient. When a circus came and
went, it left us all burning to become clowns; the first negro minstrel
show that came to our section left us all suffering to try that kind
of life; now and then we had a hope that if we lived and were good,
God would permit us to be pirates. These ambitions faded out, each
in its turn; but the ambition to be a steamboatman always remained.

Life on the Mississippi (1883)

His maxims were full of animosity toward boys. Nowadays a boy cannot follow out a single natural instinct without tumbling over some of those everlasting aphorisms and hearing from Franklin on the spot. If he buys two cents' worth of peanuts, his father says, "Remember what Franklin has said, my son— 'A groat a day's a penny a year'" and the comfort is all gone out of those peanuts. If he wants to spin his top when he has done work, his father quotes, "Procrastination is the thief of time." If he does a virtuous action, he never gets anything for it, because "Virtue is its own reward." And that boy is hounded to death and robbed of his natural rest, because Franklin said once, in one of his inspired flights of malignity: "Early to bed and early to rise / Makes a man healthy and wealthy and wise."

As if it were any object to a boy to be healthy and wealthy and wise on such terms. The sorrow that that maxim has cost me, through my parents, experimenting on me with it, tongue cannot tell. The legitimate result is my present state of general debility, indigence, and mental aberration. My parents used to have me up before nine o'clock in the morning sometimes when I was a boy. If they had let me take my natural rest where would I have been now? Keeping store, no doubt, and respected by all.

"The Late Benjamin Franklin" (1870)

There comes a time in every rightly-constructed boy's life when he has a raging desire to go somewhere and dig for hidden treasure.

The Adventures of Tom Sawyer (1876)

Well, it was a beautiful life, a lovely life. There was no crime. Merely little things like pillaging orchards and watermelon-patches and breaking the Sabbath—we didn't break the Sabbath often enough to signify—once a week perhaps. But we were good boys, all Presbyterian boys, and loyal and all that; anyway, we were good Presbyterian boys when the weather was doubtful; when it was fair, we did wander a little from the fold.

Speech, "Sixty-Seventh Birthday" (November 28, 1902)

Schoolboy days are no happier than the days of after life, but we look back upon them regretfully because we have forgotten our punishments at school, and how we grieved when our marbles were lost and our kites destroyed— because we have forgotten all the sorrows and privations of that canonized epoch and remember only its orchard robberies, its wooden-sword pageants, and its fishing holidays.

The Innocents Abroad (1869)

Familiarity breeds contempt—and children.

Notebook (1894)

I feel for Adam and Eve now, for I know how it was with them . . .
The Garden of Eden I now know was an unendurable solitude.
I know that the advent of the serpent was a welcome change—
anything for society.

Mark Twain, a Biography, Albert Bigelow Paine (1912)

Love seems the swiftest, but it is the slowest of all growths.
No man or woman really knows what perfect love is until
they have been married a quarter of a century.

Mark Twain's Notebook

Grief can take care of itself, but to get the full value of
joy you must have somebody to divide it with.

Following the Equator: A Journey Around the World (1897)

> . . . women cannot receive even the most palpably judicious
> suggestion without arguing it; that is, married women.

"Experiences of the McWilliamses with Membraneous Croup" (1875)

If you will stop and think a minute—if you will go back fifty or one
hundred years to your early married life and recontemplate your first
baby—you will remember that he amounted to a good deal and even
something over. You soliders all know that when that little fellow
arrived at family headquarters you had to hand in your resignation.
He took entire command. You became his lackey, his mere body-
servant, and you had to stand around too. He was not a commander
who made allowances for time, distance, weather, or anything
else. You had to execute his order whether it was possible or not.
And there was only one form of marching in his manual of tactics,
and that was the double-quick. He treated you with every sort of
insolence and disrespect, and the bravest of you didn't dare to say a
word. You could face the death-storm at Donelson and Vicksburg,
and give back blow for blow; but when he clawed your whiskers,
and pulled your hair, and twisted your nose, you had to take it.

Speech, "The Babies" (November 1879)

A soiled baby with a neglected nose cannot be conscientiously regarded as a thing of beauty.

"Answers to Correspondents" (1875)

It is a wise child that knows its own father, and an unusual one that unreservedly approves of him.

More Maxims of Mark, Merle Johnson (1927)

When I was a boy of 14, my father was so ignorant I could hardly stand to have the old man around. But when I got to be 21, I was astonished at how much he had learned in 7 years.

Attributed, *Reader's Digest* (September 1937)

[Of Jane Clemens, Mark Twain's mother]: Her sense of pity was abnormal. . . . She would drown the young kittens, when necessary, but warmed the water for the purpose.

Mark Twain, a Biography, Albert Bigelow Paine (1912)

It takes much to convince the average man of anything; and perhaps nothing can ever make him realize that he is the average woman's inferior—yet in several important details the evidence seems to show that that is what he is. Man has ruled the human race from the beginning—but he should remember that up to the middle of the present century it was a dull world, and ignorant and stupid; but it is not such a dull world now, and is growing less and less dull all the time.

Following the Equator: A Journey Around the World (1897)

I don't know what to tell you girls to do. Mr. Martin has told you everything you ought to do, and now I must give you some don'ts.

There are three things which come to my mind which I consider excellent advice:

First, girls, don't smoke—that is, don't smoke to excess. I am seventy-three and a half years old, and have been smoking seventy-three of them. But I never smoke to excess—that is, I smoke in moderation, only one cigar at a time.

Second, don't drink—that is, don't drink to excess.

Third, don't marry—I mean, to excess.

Speech, "Advice to Girls" (June 10, 1909)

What, sir, would the people of the earth be without woman?
They would be scarce, sir, almighty scarce.

Speech, "Woman—An Opinion" (date unknown)

. . . when we were living in Tedworth Square, London, a report was cabled to the American journals that I was dying. . . . The London representatives of the American papers began to flock in, with American cables in their hands, to inquire into my condition. There was nothing the matter with me, and each in his turn was astonished and disappointed . . . One of these was a gentle and kindly and grave and sympathetic Irishman, who hid his sorrow the best he could, and tried to look glad, and told me that his paper . . . had cabled him that it was reported in New York that I was dead. What should he cable in reply? I said—

"Say the report is greatly exaggerated."

My Autobiography (1907)

The election makes me think of a story of a man who was dying. He had only two minutes to live, so he sent for a clergyman and asked him "Where is the best place to go?" He was undecided about it. So the minister told him that each place had its advantages—heaven for climate, and hell for society.

Speech, "Tammany and Croker" (October 7, 1901)

[Satan]: " . . . there is nothing about man that is not strange to an immortal. . . . For instance, take this sample: he has imagined a heaven, and has left entirely out of it the supremest of all his delights, the one ecstasy that stands first and foremost in the heart of every individual of his race—and ours—sexual intercourse! It is as if a lost and perishing person in a roasting desert should be told by a rescuer he might choose and have all longed for things but one, and he should elect to leave out water!"

Letters from the Earth (1962)

A distinguished man should be as particular about his last words as he is about his last breath. He should write them out on a slip of paper and take the judgment of his friends on them. He should never leave such a thing to the last hour of his life, and trust to an intellectual spirit at the last moment to enable him to say something smart with his latest gasp and launch into eternity with grandeur. No—a man is apt to be too much fagged and exhausted, both in

MARK TWAIN

body and mind, at such a time, to be reliable; and maybe the very thing he wants to say, he cannot think of to save him; and besides there are his weeping friends bothering around; and worse than all as likely as not he may have to deliver his last gasp before he is expecting to. A man cannot always expect to think of a natty thing to say under such circumstances, and so it is pure egotistic ostentation to put it off. There is hardly a case on record where a man came to his last moment unprepared and said a good thing— hardly a case where a man trusted to that last moment and did not make a solemn botch of it and go out of the world feeling absurd.

"Last Words of a Great Man" (1869)

I would like to live in Manchester, England. The transition between Manchester and death would be unnoticeable.

(Attributed)

I heard the dim hum of a spinning wheel wailing along up and sinking along down again; and then I knowed for certain I wished I was dead—for that *is* the lonesomest sound in the whole world.

Adventures of Huckleberry Finn (1884)

This is my last appearance on the paid platform.
I shall not retire from the gratis platform until I am buried,
and courtesy will compel me to keep still and not disturb the others.

Speech, "Robert Fulton Fund" (April 19, 1906)

[My relations] said they had intended to give me a good send-off
when I died; but if I didn't like the flowers they wouldn't send any.
I told them that was all right. I'd rather have ice anyhow.

Interview, "The Start for Germany," *New York Times* (April 12, 1878)

Eternal Rest sounds comforting in the pulpit. . . . Well, you try it
once and see how heavy time will hang on your hands.

"Extract from Captain Stormfield's Visit to Heaven" (1909)

Where a blood relation sobs, an intimate friend should choke up,
a distant acquaintance should sigh, a stranger should merely fumble
sympathetically with his handkerchief.

Letters from the Earth (1962)

MARK TWAIN

Let us endeavor so to live that when we come
to die even the undertaker will be sorry.

The Tragedy of Pudd'nhead Wilson (1894)

It is 13 days. I am bewildered and must remain so for a
time longer. It was so sudden, so unexpected. Imagine a
man worth a hundred millions who finds himself suddenly
penniless and fifty million in debt in his old age.
I was richer than any other person in the world,
and now I am that pauper without peer.
Some day I will tell you about it, not now.

Letter on the death of his wife Livy (June 18, 1904)

The human race consists of the damned
and the ought-to-be-damned.

Mark Twain's Notebook (1898)

I have no color prejudices nor caste prejudices nor creed prejudices. All I care to know is that a man is a human being, and that is enough for me; he can't be any worse.

"Concerning the Jews" (1899)

Man adapted to the earth? Why, he can't sleep out-of-doors without freezing to death or getting the rheumatism or the malaria; he can't keep his nose under water over a minute without being drowned; he can't climb a tree without falling out and breaking his neck. Why, he's the poorest, clumsiest excuse of all the creatures that inhabit this earth. He has got to be coddled and housed and swathed and bandaged and upholstered to be able to live at all. He is a rickety sort of a thing, anyway you take him, a regular British Museum of infirmities and inferiorities. He is always undergoing repairs . . .

Mark Twain, a Biography, Albert Bigelow Paine (1912)

Man, "know thyself"—then thou wilt despise thyself to a dead moral certainty.

Letter (August 21, 1884)

When we remember we are all mad, the mysteries
of life disappear and life stands explained.

Mark Twain's Notebook (1935)

Adam was but human—this explains it all.
He did not want the apple for the apple's sake,
he wanted it only because it was forbidden.
The mistake was in not forbidding the serpent;
then he would have eaten the serpent.

The Tragedy of Pudd'nhead Wilson (1894)

A human being has a natural desire to have
more of a good thing than he needs.

Following the Equator: A Journey Around the World (1897)

Man is the only animal that blushes. Or needs to.

"The Mysterious Stranger" (1916)

[Satan]: "No brute ever does a cruel thing—
that is the monopoly of those with the moral sense.
When a brute inflicts pain he does it innocently;
it is not wrong; for him there is no such thing as wrong.
And he does not inflict pain for the pleasure of inflicting it—
only man does that."

"The Mysterious Stranger" (1916)

The holy passion of Friendship is of so sweet and steady and loyal
and enduring a nature that it will last through a whole lifetime,
if not asked to lend money.

The Tragedy of Pudd'nhead Wilson (1894)

It takes your enemy and your friend,
working together, to hurt you to the heart:
the one to slander you and the other to get the news to you.

"Pudd'nhead Wilson's New Calendar," *Following the Equator* (1897)

This is just the way in this world;
an enemy can partly ruin a man,
but it takes a good-natured injudicious friend to
complete the thing and make it perfect.

The Tragedy of Pudd'nhead Wilson (1894)

The proper office of a friend is to side with you when you are in the
wrong. Nearly anybody will side with you when you are in the right.

Mark Twain's Notebook

CLOTHING, FOOD, AND DRINK

Why don't you ask why I am wearing such apparently unseasonable clothes? I'll tell you. I have found that when a man reaches the advanced age of seventy-one years, as I have, the continual sight of dark clothing is likely to have a depressing effect upon him. Light-colored clothing is more pleasing to the eye and enlivens the spirit. Now, of course, I cannot compel everyone to wear such clothing just for my especial benefit, so I do the next best thing and wear it myself.

Speech, "Dress Reform and Copyright" (c. 1906)

Clothes make the man.
Naked people have little or no influence in society.
More Maxims of Mark, Merle Johnson (1927)

To a man all things are possible but one—he cannot have a hole
in the seat of his breeches and keep his fingers out of it.
A man does seem to feel more distress and more persistent
and distracting solicitude about such a thing than he
could about a sick child that was threatening to grow
worse every time he took his attention away from it.
Letter (June 27, 1878)

Perhaps no bread in the world is quite as good as
Southern corn bread, and perhaps no bread in the world
is quite so bad as the Northern imitation of it.
My Autobiography (1907)

The true Southern watermelon is a boon apart,
and not to be mentioned with commoner things.
It is chief of this world's luxuries,

king by the grace of God over all the fruits of the earth.
When one has tasted it, he knows what the angels eat.
It was not a Southern watermelon that Eve took:
we know it because she repented.

"Pudd'nhead Wilson's Calendar,"
The Tragedy of Pudd'nhead Wilson (1894)

Dear, dear, a body don't know what real misery is till
he is thirsty all the way through and is certain he ain't
ever going to come to any water any more.

Tom Sawyer Abroad (1894)

A banquet is probably the most fatiguing thing in the world except
ditch-digging. It is the insanest of all recreations. The inventor
of it overlooked no detail that could furnish weariness, distress,
harassment, and acute and long-sustained misery of mind and body.

Autobiography (July-August 1907)

It seems a pity that the world should throw away so many good
things merely because they are unwholesome. I doubt if God

has given us any refreshment which, taken in moderation, is unwholesome, except microbes. Yet there are people who strictly deprive themselves of each and every eatable, drinkable, and smokable which has in any way acquired a shady reputation. They pay this price for health. And health is all they get for it. How strange it is; it is like paying out your whole fortune for a cow that has gone dry.

My Autobiography (1907)

In the matter of diet . . . I have been persistently strict in sticking to the things which didn't agree with me until one or the other of us got the best of it.

Speech, "Seventieth Birthday" (December 5, 1905)

One should not bring sympathy to a sick man. It is always kindly meant, and of course it has to be taken—but it isn't much of an improvement on castor oil. One who has a sick man's true interest at heart will forbear spoken sympathy, and bring him surreptitious soup and fried oysters and other trifles that the doctor has tabooed.

Letter (February 20, 1868)

Ours was a reasonably comfortable ship, with the customary sea-going fare—plenty of good food furnished by the Deity and cooked by the devil.

Following the Equator: A Journey Around the World (1897)

Vienna coffee! It was the first thing I thought of—that unapproachable luxury—that sumptuous coffee-house coffee, compared with which all other European coffee and all American hotel coffee is mere fluid poverty.

"At the Appetite Cure" (1899)

GLOBETROTTING AND LANGUAGE

I loathe all travel, except on foot.

Letter (August 1878)

Now, the true charm of pedestrianism does not lie in the walking, or in the scenery, but in the talking. The walking is good to time the movement of the tongue by, and to keep the blood and the brain stirred up and active; the scenery and the woodsy smells are good to bear in upon a man an unconscious and unobtrusive charm and solace to eye and soul and sense; but the supreme pleasure comes from the talk. It is no matter whether one talks wisdom or nonsense, the case is the same, the bulk of the enjoyment lies in the wagging of the gladsome jaw and the flapping of the sympathetic ear.

And what a motley variety of subjects a couple of people will casually rake over in the course of a day's tramp! There being no constraint, a change of subject is always in order, and so a body is not likely to keep pegging at a single topic until it grows tiresome. We discussed everything we knew, during the first fifteen or twenty minutes that morning and then branched out into the glad, free, boundless realm of the things we were not certain about.

A Tramp Abroad (1880)

I have found out that there ain't no surer way to find out whether
you like people or hate them than to travel with them.

Tom Sawyer Abroad (1894)

The gentle reader will never, never know what a
consummate ass he can become until he goes abroad.

The Innocents Abroad (1869)

It's spring fever. That is what the name of it is. And when you've got
it, you want—oh, you don't quite know what it is you *do* want, but
it just fairly makes your heart ache, you want it so! It seems to you
that mainly what you want is to get away; get away from the same
old tedious things you're so used to seeing and so tired of, and see
something new. That is the idea; you want to go and be a wanderer;
you want to go wandering far away to strange countries where
everything is mysterious and wonderful and romantic. And if you
can't do that, you'll put up with considerable less; you'll go anywhere
you *can* go, just so as to get away, and be thankful of the chance, too.

Tom Sawyer, Detective (1896)

There have always been ruins, no doubt; and there have always been pensive people to sigh over them, and asses to scratch upon them their names and the important date of their visit. Within a hundred years after Adam left Eden, the guide probably gave the usual general flourish with his hand and said: "Place where the animals were named, ladies and gentlemen; place where the tree of the forbidden fruit stood; exact spot where Adam and Eve first met; and here, ladies and gentlemen, adorned and hallowed by the names and addresses of Cain's altar—fine old ruin!" Then, no doubt, he taxed them a shekel apiece and let them go.

A Tramp Abroad (1880)

A long sea-voyage not only brings out all the mean traits one has, and exaggerates them, but raises up others which he never suspected he possessed, and even creates new ones.

The Innocents Abroad (1869)

If there is one thing that will make a man peculiarly and insufferably self-conceited, it is to have his stomach behave itself, the first day at sea, when nearly all his comrades are seasick.

The Innocents Abroad (1869)

I go by water, because I don't like the railroads.
I wouldn't go to heaven by rail if the chance was offered me.

Interview, "Mark Twain's Travels,"
St. Louis Globe-Democrat (May 13, 1882)

People wonder why I go [to England] so much. Well, I go partly for my health, partly to familiarize myself with the road. I have gone over the same road so many times now that I know all the whales that belong along the route, and latterly it is an embarrassment to me to meet them, for they do not look glad to see me, but annoyed, and they seem to say, "Here is this old derelict again."

Earlier in life this would have pained me and made me ashamed, but I am older now, and when I am behaving myself, and doing right, I do not care for a whale's opinion about me. When we are young we generally estimate an opinion by the size of the person that holds it, but later we find that that is an uncertain rule, for we realize that there are times when a hornet's opinion disturbs us more than an emperor's.

I do not mean that I care nothing at all for a whale's opinion, for that would be going to too great a length. Of course, it is better to have the good opinion of a whale than his disapproval; but my position is that if you cannot have a whale's good opinion, except at some sacrifice of principle or personal dignity, it is better to try to live without it.

Speech, "An Undelivered Speech" (March 25, 1895)

An indefatigable traveler! That's where I am misunderstood. Now I have made thirty-four long journeys in my life, and thirty-two of them were made under the spur of absolute compulsion. I mean it—under nothing but sheer compulsion. There always was an imperative reason. I had to gather material for books or sketches, I had to stump around lecturing to make money, or I had to go abroad for the health or the education of my family. For love of travel—never any of these thirty-two journeys. There is no man living who cares less about seeing new places and peoples than I. You are surprised—but it's the gospel truth. I had a surfeit of it.

Interview, *New York World* (October 14, 1900)

You perceive I generalize with intrepidity from single instances. It is the tourist's custom.

Mark Twain's Notebooks (no date)

MARK TWAIN

To be the *first*—that is the idea. To do something, say something, see something, before *anybody* else—these are the things that confer a pleasure compared with which other pleasures are tame and commonplace, other ecstasies cheap and trivial.

The Innocents Abroad (1869)

. . . we were the same sort of simpletons as those who climb unnecessarily the perilous peaks of Mont Blanc and the Matterhorn, and derive no pleasure from it except the reflection that it isn't a common experience.

Roughing It (1872)

. . . a man who keeps company with glaciers comes to feel tolerably insignificant by and by. The Alps and the glaciers together are able to take every bit of conceit out of a man and reduce his self-importance to zero if he will only remain within the influence of their sublime presence long enough to give it a fair and reasonable chance to do its work.

A Tramp Abroad (1880)

Nothing is gained in the Alps by over-exertion; nothing is gained by crowding two days' work into one for the poor sake of being able to boast of the exploit afterward. It will be found much better, in the long run, to do the thing in two days, and then subtract one of them from the narrative. This saves fatigue, and does not injure the narrative. All the more thoughtful among the Alpine tourists do this.

A Tramp Abroad (1880)

[Family hotels] are a London speciality, God has not permitted them to exist elsewhere. . . . All the modern inconveniences are furnished, and some that have been obsolete for a century. . . . The bedrooms are hospitals for incurable furniture.

Letter (September 1900)

Perhaps most of them were not always reverent during that Holy Land trip. It was a trying journey, and after fierce days of desert hills the reaction might not always spare even the holiest memories. Jack was particularly sinful. When they learned the price for a boat on Galilee, and the deacons who

had traveled nearly half around the world to sail on that
sacred water were confounded by the charge, Jack said:
"Well, Denny, do you wonder now that Christ walked?"

Mark Twain, a Biography, Albert Bigelow Paine (1912)

There is the Sea of Galilee and this Dead Sea—neither of them
twenty miles long or thirteen wide. And yet when I was in Sunday-
school I thought they were sixty thousand miles in diameter.
Travel and experience mar the grandest pictures and rob
us of the most cherished traditions of our boyhood.

The Innocents Abroad (1869)

This is indeed India; the land of dreams and romance, of fabulous
wealth and fabulous poverty, of splendor and rags, of palaces and
hovels, of famine and pestilence, of genii and giants and Aladdin
lamps, of tigers and elephants, the cobra and the jungle, the country
of a hundred nations and a hundred tongues, of a thousand religions
and two million gods, cradle of the human race, birthplace of human
speech, mother of history, grandmother of legend, great-

grandmother of tradition, whose yesterdays bear date with the moldering antiquities of the rest of the nations—the one sole country under the sun that is endowed with an imperishable interest for alien prince and alien peasant, for lettered and ignorant, wise and fool, rich and poor, bond and free, the one land that *all* men desire to see, and having seen once, by even a glimpse, would not give that glimpse for the shows of all the rest of the globe combined.

Following the Equator: A Journey Around the World (1897)

In India "cold weather" is merely a conventional phrase and has come into use through the necessity of having some way to distinguish between weather which will melt a brass door-knob and weather which will only make it mushy.

Following the Equator: A Journey Around the World (1897)

For ever and ever the memory of my distant first glimpse of the Taj [Mahal] will compensate me for creeping around the globe to have that great privilege.

Following the Equator: A Journey Around the World (1897)

. . . Nature is always stingy of perfect climates; stingier in the case of Australia than usual. Apparently, this vast continent has a really good climate nowhere but around the edges.

Following the Equator: A Journey Around the World (1897)

There are several "sights" in the Bermudas, of course, but they are easily avoided. This is a great advantage—one cannot have it in Europe.

Some Rambling Notes of an Idle Excursion (1878)

The Sandwich Islands remain my ideal of the perfect thing in the matter of tropical islands. I would add another story to Mauna Loa's sixteen thousand feet if I could, and make it particularly bold and steep and craggy and forbidding and snowy; and I would make the volcano spout its lava-floods out of its summit instead of its sides; but aside from these non-essentials I have no corrections to suggest. I hope these will be attended to; I do not wish to have to speak of it again.

Following the Equator: A Journey Around the World (1897)

Travel has no longer any charm for me. I have seen all the
foreign countries I want to see except heaven and hell,
and I have only a vague curiosity as concerns one of those.

Letter (May 20, 1891)

In the museums you will find acres of the most strange
and fascinating things; but all museums are fascinating,
and they do so tire your eyes, and break your back,
and burn out your vitalities with their consuming interest.
You always say you will never go again but you do go.

Following the Equator: A Journey Around the World (1897)

Homesickness was abroad in the ship—it was epidemic.
If the authorities of New York had known how badly we had it,
they would have quarantined us here.

The Innocents Abroad (1869)

It has always been a marvel to me—that French language;
it has always been a puzzle to me. How beautiful that language is!
How expressive it seems to be! How full of grace it is!
And when it comes from lips like those [of Sarah Bernhardt],
how eloquent and how limpid it is! And, oh, I am always
deceived—I always think I am going to understand it.

Mark Twain, a Biography, Albert Bigelow Paine (1912)

French is not a familiar tongue to me, and the pronunciation
is difficult, and comes out of me encumbered with a Missouri
accent; but the cats like it, and when I make impassioned
speeches in that language they sit in a row and put up
their paws, palm to palm, and frantically give thanks.

Mark Twain's Autobiography

I heard a Californian student in Heidelberg say,
in one of his calmest moods, that he would rather
decline two drinks than one German adjective.

A Tramp Abroad (1880)

The Germans have an inhuman way of cutting up their verbs.
Now a verb has a hard time enough of it in this world when
it's all together. It's downright inhuman to split it up. But
that's just what those Germans do. They take part of a verb
and put it down here, like a stake, and they take the other
part of it and put it away over yonder like another stake, and
between these two limits they just shoved in German.

Speech, "Disappearance of Literature" (November 20, 1900)

I have heard of an American student who was asked how he was
getting along with his German, and who answered promptly:
"I am not getting along at all. I have worked on it hard for three
level months, and all I have got to show for it is one solitary German
phrase— *'Zwei glas,'* " (two glasses of beer). He paused a moment,
reflectively, then added with feeling, "But I've got that *solid!*"

A Tramp Abroad (1880)

My philological studies have satisfied me that a gifted person ought to learn English (barring spelling and pronouncing) in thirty hours, French in thirty days, and German in thirty years. It seems manifest, then, that the latter tongue ought to be trimmed down and repaired. If it is to remain as it is, it ought to be gently and reverently set aside among the dead languages, for only the dead have time to learn it.

"The Awful German Language," *A Tramp Abroad* (1880)

I can *understand* German as well as the maniac that invented it, but I *talk* it best through an interpreter.

A Tramp Abroad (1880)

GUILT, LIES, AND TRUTH

Good friends, good books and a sleepy
conscience: this is the ideal life.

Mark Twain's Notebook

. . . in my age, as in my youth, night brings me many a deep remorse. I realize that from the cradle up I have been like the rest of the race—never quite sane in the night.

My Autobiography (1907)

"All the consciences *I* have ever heard of were nagging, badgering, fault-finding, execrable savages! Yes; and always in a sweat about some poor little insignificant trifle or other—destruction catch the lot of them, *I* say! I would trade mine for the smallpox and seven kinds of consumption, and be glad of the chance. Now tell me, why *is* it that a conscience can't haul a man over the coals once, for an offense, and then let him alone? Why is it that it wants to keep on pegging at him, day and night and night and day, week in and week out, forever and ever, about the same old thing? There is no sense in that, and no reason in it. I think a conscience that will act like that is meaner than the very dirt itself."

"Crime Carnival in Connecticut" (1876)

.

It was ever thus, all through my life: whenever I have diverged from custom and principle and uttered a truth, the rule has been that the hearer hadn't strength of mind enough to believe it.

My Autobiography (1907)

Every evening I have to tell the children a story after they are in their cribs and their prayers accomplished—and the story has to be invented on the spot; neither of them will put up with any second-hand contributions. Now in all these inventions of mine, from away back, I have had one serious difficulty to contend with, owing to Alison's influence—*nobody in my tale must lie,* not even the villain of the piece. This hampers me a good deal. The blacker and bloodier I paint the villain the more the children delight in him, until he makes the mistake of telling a lie—then down he goes, in their estimation. Nothing can resurrect him again; he has to pack up and go; his character is damaged beyond help, they won't have him around any longer.

"Which Was the Dream?" (1897)

Truth is stranger than fiction, but it is because Fiction
is obliged to stick to possibilities; Truth isn't.

"Pudd'nhead Wilson's New Calendar," *Following the Equator* (1897)

When he got done telling it there was one of them uncomfortable
silences that comes, you know, when a person has been telling
a whopper and you feel sorry for him and wish you could think
of some way to change the subject and let him down easy, but
git stuck and don't see no way, and before you can pull your
mind together and do something, that silence has got in and
spread itself and done the business. I was embarrassed, Jim
he was embarrassed, and neither of us couldn't say a word.

Tom Sawyer Abroad (1894)

A man cannot tell the whole truth about himself, even if
convinced that what he wrote would never be seen by others.
I have personally satisfied myself of that and have got others to
test it also. You cannot lay bare your private soul and look at it.
You are too much ashamed of yourself. It is too disgusting. For
that reason I confine myself to drawing the portraits of others.

Interview, "Mark Twain's Bequest," *Times* of London (May 23, 1899)

MARK TWAIN

To promise not to do a thing is the surest way in the world
to make a body want to go and do that very thing.

The Adventures of Tom Sawyer (1876)

It is my belief that nearly any invented quotation,
played with confidence, stands a good chance to deceive.
There are some people who think that honesty is always
the best policy. This is a superstition; there are times
when the appearance of it is worth six of it.

Following the Equator: A Journey Around the World (1897)

The men in that far country were liars, every one.
Their mere howdy-do was a lie, because *they* didn't
care how you did, except they were undertakers.

Tom Sawyer Abroad (1894)

In all lies there is wheat among the chaff.

A Connecticut Yankee in King Arthur's Court (1889)

When he slept, he snored a lie; when he awoke,
he blinked a falsehood.

Mark Twain and I, Opie Read (1940)

The most outrageous lies that can be invented will find
believers if a man only tells them with all his might.

Mark Twain's Travels with Mr. Brown (1940)

I should be sorry to sit down without having said one
serious word which you can carry home and relate to your
children and the old people who are not able to get away.
And this is just a little maxim which has saved me from
many a difficulty and many a disaster, and in times of
tribulation and uncertainty has come to my rescue,
as it shall to yours if you observe it as I do day and night.
I always use it in an emergency, and you can take it home as a
legacy from me, and it is: "When in doubt, tell the truth."

Speech, "To the Whitefriars" (June 20, 1899)

Emotions are among the toughest things in the
world to manufacture out of whole cloth; it is easier
to manufacture seven facts than one emotion.

Life on the Mississippi (1883)

A man is never more truthful than when
he acknowledges himself a liar.

Mark Twain and I, Opie Read (1940)

When I was seven or eight, or ten, or twelve years
old—along there—a neighbor said to her,
"Do you ever believe anything that that boy says?"
My mother said, "He is the well-spring of truth, but you
can't bring up the whole well with one bucket"—and she
added, "I know his average, therefore he never deceives me.
I discount him thirty percent for embroidery, and what is left
is perfect and priceless truth, without a flaw in it anywhere."

My Autobiography (1907)

GUILT, LIES, AND TRUTH

The real life that I live, and the real life that I suppose all of you live, is a life of interior sin. That is what makes life valuable and pleasant. To lead a life of undiscovered sin! That is true joy.

Speech, "Society of American Authors" (November 15, 1900)

A sin takes on new and real terrors when there seems a chance that it is going to be found out.

"The Man That Corrupted Hadleyburg" (1900)

Man will do many things to get himself loved, he will do all things to get himself envied.

"Pudd'nhead Wilson's New Calendar," *Following the Equator* (1897)

Human pride is not worth while; there is always something lying in wait to take the wind out of it.

Following the Equator: A Journey Around the World (1897)

One never ceases to make a hero of one's self (in private).

The Gilded Age (1873)

There are people who can do all fine and heroic things but one:
keep from telling their happiness to the unhappy.
Following the Equator: A Journey Around the World (1897)

I am not as lazy as I was—but I am lazy enough yet for two people.
Letter (December 12, 1867)

I *have* seen slower people than I am—and more deliberate . . .
and even quieter and more listless and lazier people than I am.
But they were dead.
Galaxy Magazine (December 1870)

To have nothing the matter with you and no habits is pretty tame,
pretty colorless. It is just the way a saint feels, I reckon;
it is at least the way he looks. I never could stand a saint.
"Marienbad—Health Factory" (February 7, 1892)

April 1. This is the day upon which we are reminded of what we are on the other three hundred and sixty-four.

"Pudd'nhead Wilson's Calendar,"
The Tragedy of Pudd'nhead Wilson (1894)

I am no lazier than I was forty years ago, but that is because I reached the limit forty years ago. You can't go beyond possibility.

Autobiography (1922)

He is useless on top of the ground; he ought to be under it, inspiring the cabbages.

"Pudd'nhead Wilson's Calendar,"
The Tragedy of Pudd'nhead Wilson (1894)

. . . you can't depend on your eyes when your imagination is out of focus.

A Connecticut Yankee in King Arthur's Court (1889)

A photograph is a most important document, and there is nothing more damning to go down to posterity than a silly, foolish smile caught and fixed forever.

Mark Twain and the Happy Island, Elizabeth Wallace (1913)

I thoroughly disapprove of duels. I consider them unwise and I know they are dangerous. Also, sinful. If a man should challenge me now I would go to that man and take him kindly and forgivingly by the hand and lead him to a quiet retired spot and *kill* him.

My Autobiography (1907)

I like compliments. I like to go home and tell them all over again to the members of my family. They don't believe them, but I like to tell them in the home circle all the same. I like to dream of them if I can. I thank everybody for their compliments, but I don't think that I am praised any more than I am entitled to be.

Speech, "Society of American Authors" (November 15, 1900)

In certain trying circumstances, urgent circumstances, desperate circumstances, profanity furnishes a relief denied even to prayer.

Mark Twain, a Biography, Albert Bigelow Paine (1912)

The existing [Italian] phrase-books are inadequate. They are well enough as far as they go, but when you fall down and skin your leg they don't tell you what to say.

"Italian without a Master" (1903)

Don't imagine that I have lost my temper, because I swear. I swear all day, but I do not lose my temper. And don't imagine that I am on my way to the poorhouse, for I am not; or that I am uneasy, for I am not, or that I am uncomfortable or unhappy— for I never am. I don't know what it is to be unhappy or uneasy; and I am not going to try to learn how, at this late day.

Letter to his brother Orion (November 29, 1888)

It takes me a long time to lose my temper, but once lost I could not find it with a dog.

Mark Twain's Notebook

MARK TWAIN

All through the first ten years of my married life I kept a constant and discreet watch upon my tongue while in the house, and went outside and to a distance when circumstances were too much for me and I was obliged to seek relief. I prized my wife's respect and approval above all the rest of the human race's respect and approval. I dreaded the day when she should discover that I was but a whited sepulchre partly freighted with suppressed language.

My Autobiography (1907)

I was . . . blaspheming my luck in a way that made my breath smell of brimstone.

Roughing It (1872)

If I cannot swear in heaven I shall not stay there.

Mark Twain's Notebook

HISTORY AND CIVILIZATION

It is not worthwhile to try to keep history from repeating itself, for man's character will always make the preventing of the repetitions impossible.

Mark Twain in Eruption (1940)

The battle of Waterloo was fought on the 18th of June, 1815. I do not state this fact as a reminder to the reader, but as news to him. For a forgotten fact *is* news when it comes again. Writers of books have the fashion of whizzing by vast and renowned historical events with the remark, "The details of this tremendous episode are too familiar to the reader to need repeating here." They know that that is not true. It is a low kind of flattery. They know that the reader has forgotten every detail of it, and that nothing of the tremendous event is left in his mind but a vague and formless luminous smudge. Aside from the desire to flatter the reader, they have another reason for making the remark—two reasons, indeed. They do not remember the details themselves, and do not want the trouble of hunting them up and copying them out; also, they are afraid that if they search them out and print them they will be scoffed at by the book-reviewers for retelling those worn old things which are familiar to everybody. They should not mind the reviewer's jeer; *he* doesn't remember any of the worn old things until the book which he is reviewing has retold them to him.

Following the Equator: A Journey Around the World (1897)

Later ancestors of mine were the Quakers William Robinson, Marmaduke Stevenson, *et al.* Your tribe chased them out of the country for their religion's sake; promised them death if they came back; for your ancestors had forsaken the homes they loved, and braved the perils of the sea, the implacable climate, and the savage wilderness to acquire that highest and most precious of boons, freedom for every man on this broad continent to worship according to the dictates of his own conscience—and they were not going to allow a lot of pestiferous Quakers to interfere with it. Your ancestors broke forever the chains of political slavery, and gave the vote to every man in the wide land, excluding none!—none except those who did not belong to the orthodox church. Your ancestors—yes, they were a hard lot; but, nevertheless, they gave us religious liberty to worship as they required us to worship, and political liberty to vote as the church required; and so I the bereft one, I the forlorn one, am here to do my best to help you celebrate them right.

Speech, "Plymouth Rock and the Pilgrims" (December 22, 1881)

A historian who would convey the truth has got to lie.
Often he must enlarge the truth by diameters,
otherwise his reader would not be able to see it.

Mark Twain, a Biography, Albert Bigelow Paine (1912)

Civilization is a limitless multiplication of unnecessary necessaries.

More Maxims of Mark, Merle Johnson (1927)

We can easily perceive that the peoples furthest from
civilization are the ones where equality between man and
woman are furthest apart—and we consider this one of the
signs of savagery. But we are so stupid that we can't see that
we thus plainly admit that no civilization can be perfect until
exact equality between man and woman is included.

Mark Twain's Notebook (1895)

. . . the coat of arms of the human race ought to consist of a
man with an ax on his shoulder proceeding toward a grindstone,
or it ought to represent the several members of the human race
holding out the hat to one another; for we are all beggars, each

in his own way. One beggar is too proud to beg for pennies, but will beg for an introduction into society; another does not care for society, but he wants a postmastership; another will inveigle a lawyer into conversation and then sponge on him for free advice. The man who wouldn't do any of these things will beg for the Presidency. Each admires his own dignity and greatly guards it, but in his opinion the others haven't any. Mendicancy is a matter of taste and temperament, no doubt.

Mark Twain, a Biography, Albert Bigelow Paine (1912)

There are many humorous things in the world; among them, the white man's notion that he is less savage than the other savages.

Following the Equator: A Journey Around the World (1897)

In more than one country we have hunted the savage and his little children and their mother with dogs and guns through the woods and swamps for an afternoon's sport, and filled the region with happy laughter over their sprawling and stumbling flight, and their wild supplications for mercy; but this method we do not mind, because custom has inured us to it; yet a quick death by poison is loving-kindness to it. In many countries we have taken the savage's land from him, and made him our slave, and lashed him every day, and broken his pride, and made death his only friend, and overworked him till he dropped in his tracks; and this we do not care for, because custom has inured us to it; yet a quick death by poison is loving-kindness to it.

Following the Equator: A Journey Around the World (1897)

The Whites always mean well when they take human fish out of the ocean and try to make them dry and warm and happy and comfortable in a chicken coop; but the kindest-hearted white man can always be depended on to prove himself inadequate when he deals with savages. He cannot turn the situation around and imagine how he would like it to have a well-meaning savage transfer him from his house and his church and his clothes and his books and his choice food to a hideous wilderness of sand and rocks and snow, and ice and sleet and storm and blistering sun, with no shelter, no bed, no covering for his and his family's naked bodies, and nothing to eat but snakes and grubs and offal. This would be a hell to him; and if he had any wisdom he would know that his own civilization is a hell to the savage—but he hasn't any, and has never had any; and for lack of it he shut up those poor natives in the unimaginable perdition of his civilization, committing his crime with the very best intentions, and saw those poor creatures waste away under his tortures; and gazed at it, vaguely troubled and sorrowful, and wondered what could be the matter with them.

Following the Equator: A Journey Around the World (1897)

And it seemed an epitome of war; that all war must be just that— the killing of strangers against whom you feel no personal animosity; strangers whom, in other circumstances, you would help if you found them in trouble, and who help you if you needed it.

"The Private History of a Campaign That Failed" (1885)

"You perceive," [Satan] said, "that you have made continual progress. Cain did his murder with a club; the Hebrews did their murders with javelins and swords; the Greeks and Romans added protective armor and the fine arts of military organization and generalship; the Christian has added guns and gunpowder; a few centuries from now he will have so greatly improved the deadly effectiveness of his weapons of slaughter that all men will confess that without Christian civilization war must have remained a poor and trifling thing to the end of time."

"The Mysterious Stranger" (1916)

I have been reading the morning paper. I do it every morning—well knowing that I shall find in it the usual depravities and basenesses and hypocrisies and cruelties that make up civilization, and cause me to put in the rest of the day pleading for the damnation of the human race.

Letter (April 6, 1899)

Peace by compulsion. That seems a better idea than the other. Peace by persuasion has a pleasant sound, but I think we should not be able to work it. We should have to tame the human race first, and history seems to show that that cannot be done.

Letter (January 9, 1899)

We ought never to do wrong when people are looking.

"A Double-Barreled Detective Story" (1902)

"Thou shalt not commit adultery" is a command which makes no distinction between the following persons. They are all required to obey it: children at birth. Children in the cradle. School children. Youths and maidens. Fresh adults. Older ones. Men and women of 40. Of 50. Of 60. Of 70. Of 80. Of 90. Of 100. The command does not distribute its burden equally, and cannot. It is not hard upon the three sets of children.

Letters from the Earth (1962)

We have a criminal jury system which is superior to any in the world; and its efficiency is only marred by the difficulty of finding twelve men every day who don't know anything and can't read. And I may observe that we have an insanity plea that would have saved Cain. I think I can say, and say with pride, that we have some legislatures that bring higher prices than any in the world.

"The Fourth of July" (1875)

There was absolutely no semblance of law there. Violence was the rule. Force was the only recognized authority. The commonest misunderstandings were settled on the spot with the revolver or the knife. Murders were done in open day, and with sparkling frequency, and nobody thought of inquiring into them. It was considered that all parties who did the killing had their private reasons for it; for other people to meddle would have been looked upon as indelicate. After a murder, all that Rocky Mountain etiquette required of a spectator was, that he should help the gentleman bury his game—otherwise his churlishness would surely be remembered against him the first time he killed a man himself and needed a neighborly turn in interring him.

Roughing It (1872)

As an active privilege, [free speech] ranks with the privilege of committing murder: we may exercise it if we are willing to take the consequences. Murder is forbidden both in form and in fact. By the common estimate both are crimes, and are held in deep odium by all civilized people. Murder is sometimes punished, free speech always—when committed. Which is seldom.

"The Privilege of the Grave" (September 18, 1905)

MARK TWAIN

Men write many fine and plausible arguments in support
of monarchy, but the fact remains that where every man
in a state has a vote, brutal laws are impossible.

A Connecticut Yankee in King Arthur's Court (1889)

Let me make the superstitions of a nation and I care
not who makes its laws or its songs either.

"Pudd'nhead Wilson's New Calendar," *Following the Equator* (1897)

In my schoolboy days I had no aversion to slavery. I was not
aware that there was anything wrong about it. No one arraigned
it in my hearing; the local papers said nothing against it;
the local pulpit taught us that God approved it, that it was a
holy thing, and that the doubter need only look in the Bible
if he wished to settle his mind—and then the texts were read
aloud to us to make the matter sure; if the slaves themselves
had an aversion to slavery they were wise and said nothing.

My Autobiography (1907)

HUMOR

There are several kinds of stories, but only one difficult kind—the humorous. I will talk mainly about that one. The humorous story is American, the comic story is English, the witty story is French. The humorous story depends for its effect upon the *manner* of the telling; the comic story and the witty story upon the *matter*.

"How to Tell a Story" (1895)

Wit and Humor—if any difference it is in duration—lightning and electric light. Same material, apparently; but one is vivid, brief, and can do damage—the other fools along and enjoys elaboration.

Mark Twain's Notebook

I have no sense of humor. In illustration of this fact I will say this—by way of confession—that if there is a humorous passage in the *Pickwick Papers* I have never been able to find it.

Mark Twain's Notebook

There is no lasting quality to humor unless it's based on real substance. Being funny doesn't mean anything unless there is an underlying human note.
People don't realize that this requires the same powers of observation, analysis, and understanding as in serious writing.

Celebrities Off Parade, William Orcutt (1935)

It takes a heap of sense to write good nonsense.
Mark Twain's Notebooks (c. 1879)

Somebody has said "Wit is the sudden marriage of ideas which before their union were not perceived to have any relation."
Mark Twain's Notebook

To string incongruities and absurdities together in a wandering and sometimes purposeless way, and seem innocently unaware that they are absurdities, is the basis of the American art . . .
"How to Tell a Story" (1895)

Laughter without a tinge of philosophy is but a sneeze of humor. Genuine humor is replete with wisdom.
Mark Twain and I, Opie Read (1940)

. . . humor is the great thing, the saving thing, after all.
The minute it crops up all our hardnesses yield,
all our irritations and resentments slip away,
and a sunny spirit takes their place.

"What Paul Bourget Thinks of Us" (1895)

The pun is like mediocre music, neither wit nor
humor—and yet now and then one sees a pun which
comes so near being wit that it is funny.

Mark Twain's Notebooks and Journals (c. 1878)

Humor is serious. When you sit down to write humor go
at it seriously; if the humor doesn't come, don't write it.

Interview, *New York Sun* (October 16, 1900)

. . . I have witnessed and greatly enjoyed the first act of everything which Wagner created, but the effect on me has always been so powerful that one act was quite sufficient; whenever I have witnessed two acts I have gone away physically exhausted; and whenever I have ventured an entire opera the result has been the next thing to suicide.

Autobiography (November 30, 1906)

LITERATURE AND EDUCATION

Books are the liberated spirits of men.

Letter (February 1894)

Professor Winchester . . . said something about there being no modern epics like *Paradise Lost*. I guess he's right. He talked as if he was pretty familiar with that piece of literary work, and nobody would suppose that he never had read it. I don't believe any of you have ever read *Paradise Lost,* and you don't want to. That's something that you just want to take on trust. It's a classic, just as Professor Winchester says, and it meets his definition of a classic—something that everybody wants to have read and nobody wants to read.

Speech, "Disappearance of Literature" (November 20, 1900)

A big leather-bound volume makes an ideal razorstrap. A thin book is useful to stick under a table with a broken caster to steady it. A large, flat atlas can be used to cover a window with a broken pane. And a thick, old-fashioned heavy book with a clasp is the finest thing in the world to throw at a noisy cat.

(Unknown source)

You ask me where I spend my evenings. Where would you suppose, with a free printers' library containing more than 4,000 volumes within a quarter of a mile of me and nobody at home to talk to?

Letter to his sister (Summer 1853)

An author values a compliment even when it comes
from a source of doubtful competency.

Autobiography (June 1, 1906)

It is hard to make a choice of the most beautiful passage in a book
which is so jammed with beautiful passages as the Bible; but it is
certain that not many things within its lids may take rank above the
exquisite story of Joseph. Who taught those ancient writers their
simplicity of language, their felicity of expression, their pathos, and
above all, their faculty of sinking themselves entirely out of sight
of the reader and making the narrative stand out alone and seem
to tell itself? Shakespeare is always present when one reads his
book; Macauley is present when we follow the march of his stately
sentences; but the Old Testament writers are hidden from view.

The Innocents Abroad (1869)

. . . you've got to be one of two ages to appreciate [Sir Walter]
Scott. When you're eighteen you can read *Ivanhoe*, and you want
to wait until you are ninety to read some of the rest. It takes a
pretty well-regulated, abstemious critic to live ninety years.

Speech, "Disappearance of Literature" (November 20, 1900)

I bored through *Middlemarch* during the past week, with its labored and tedious analyses of feelings and motives, its paltry and tiresome people, its unexciting and uninteresting story, and its frequent blinding flashes of single-sentence poetry, philosophy, wit, and what not, and nearly died from the overwork. I wouldn't read another of those books for a farm. I did try to read one other—*Daniel Deronda*. I dragged through three chapters, losing flesh all the time, and then was honest enough to quit . . .

Letter (July 21, 1885)

I can't stand George Eliot and Hawthorne and those people; I see what they are at a hundred years before they get to it and they just tire me to death. And as for [Henry James's] *The Bostonians*, I would rather be damned to John Bunyan's heaven than read that.

Letter (July 21, 1885)

Jane Austen's books, too, are absent from this library. Just that one omission alone would make a fairly good library out of a library that hadn't a book in it.

Following the Equator: A Journey Around the World (1897)

The library at the British Museum I find particularly astounding. I have read there hours together, and hardly made an impression on it. I revere that library. It is the author's friend. I don't care how mean a book is, it always takes one copy. And then every day that author goes there to gaze at that book, and is encouraged to go on in the good work.

Speech, "About London" (September 28, 1872)

[Rudyard Kipling] is a stranger to me but he is a most remarkable man—and I am the other one. Between us, we cover all knowledge; he knows all that can be known, and I know the rest.

Autobiography (August 13, 1906)

I was sorry to have my name mentioned as one of the great authors, because they have a sad habit of dying off. Chaucer is dead, Spenser is dead, so is Milton, so is Shakespeare, and I am not feeling very well myself.

Speech, "Statistics" (June 9, 1899)

Heroine: girl who is perfectly charming to live with, in a book.

More Maxims of Mark, Merle Johnson (1927)

Perhaps no poet is a conscious plagiarist; but there seems
to be warrant for suspecting that there is no poet who
is not at one time or another an unconscious one.

Following the Equator: A Journey Around the World (1897)

Names are not always what they seem. The common
Welsh name Bzjxxllwcp is pronounced Jackson.

"Pudd'nhead Wilson's New Calendar," *Following the Equator* (1897)

The Committee of the Public Library of Concord, Massachusetts,
have given us a rattling tip-top puff which will go into every paper in
the country. They have expelled *Huck* from their library as "trash and
suitable only for the slums." That will sell 25,000 copies for us sure.

Letter (March 18, 1885)

Most honestly do I wish that I could say a softening word
or two in defense of Huck's character since you wish it,
but really, in my opinion, it is no better than those of
Solomon, David and the rest of the sacred brotherhood.

Letter (undated)

But the truth is, that when a library expels a book of mine
and leaves an unexpurgated Bible lying around where
unprotected youth and age can get hold of it, the deep
unconscious irony of it delights me and doesn't anger me.

Letter (February 7, 1907)

. . . I was scared into being a city editor. I would have declined
otherwise. Necessity is the mother of "taking chances." I do
not doubt that if, at that time, I had been offered a salary to
translate the Talmud from the original Hebrew, I would have
accepted—albeit with diffidence and some misgivings—and
thrown as much variety into it as I could for the money.

Roughing It (1872)

Nobody, except he who has tried it, knows what it is to be an editor. It is easy to scribble local rubbish, with the facts all before you; it is easy to clip selections from other papers; it is easy to string out a correspondence from any locality; but it is unspeakable hardship to write editorials. *Subjects* are the trouble—the dreary lack of them, I mean. Every day, it is drag, drag, drag—think, and worry and suffer—all the world is a dull blank, and yet the editorial columns *must* be filled. Only give the editor a *subject*, and his work is done—it is no trouble to write it up; but fancy how you would feel if you had to pump your brains dry every day in the week, fifty-two weeks in the year. It makes one low-spirited simply to think of it.

Roughing It (1872)

Every man, I take it, has a selfish end in view when he pours out eloquence in behalf of the public good in the newspapers, and such is the case with me.

"Female Suffrage" (1867)

For several quite plain and simple reasons, an "interview" must, as a rule, be an absurdity, and chiefly for this reason—it is an attempt to use a boat on land or a wagon on water, to speak figuratively. Spoken speech is one thing, written speech is quite another. Print is the proper vehicle for the latter, but it isn't for the former. The moment "talk" is put into print you recognize that it is not what it was when you heard it; you perceive that an immense something has disappeared from it. That is its soul. You have nothing but a dead carcass left on your hands. Color, play of feature, the varying modulations of the voice, the laugh, the smile, the informing inflections, everything that gave that body warmth, grace, friendliness and charm and commended it to your affections—or, at least, to your tolerance—is gone and nothing is left but a pallid, stiff and repulsive cadaver.

Letter to a journalist (1888)

There is no character, howsoever good and fine, but it can be destroyed by ridicule, howsoever poor and witless.

The Tragedy of Pudd'nhead Wilson (1894)

. . . the devil's aversion to holy water is a light matter compared with a despot's dread of a newspaper that laughs.

"The American Press" (June-September 1888)

[Satan]: " . . . your race, in its poverty, has unquestionably one really effective weapon—laughter. Power, money, persuasion, supplication, persecution—these can lift at a colossal humbug—push it a little—weaken it a little, century by century; but only laughter can blow it to rags and atoms at a blast. Against the assault of laughter nothing can stand. You are always fussing and fighting with your other weapons. Do you ever use that one? No; you leave it lying rusting. As a race, do you ever use it at all? No; you lack sense and the courage."

"The Mysterious Stranger" (1916)

I believe it is our irreverent press which has laughed away, one by one, what remained of our inherited minor shams and delusions and serfages after the Revolution, and made us the only really free people that has yet existed in the earth; and I believe we shall remain free, utterly free and unassailably free, until some alien critic with sugared speech shall persuade our journalism to forsake its scoffing ways and serve itself up on the innocuous European plan. Our press has done a worthy work; is doing a worthy work; and so, though one should prove to me—a thing easily within the possibilities—that its faults are abundant and over-abundant, I should still say, no matter: so long as it still possesses that supreme virtue in journalism, an active and discriminating irreverence, it will be entitled to hold itself the most valuable press, the most wholesome press, and the most puissant force for the nurture and protection of human freedom that either hemisphere has yet produced since the printer's art set itself the tedious and disheartening task of righting the wrongs of men.

"The American Press" (June-September 1888)

The difference between the right word and the almost right word is the difference between lightning and the lightning bug.

(Attributed)

The thought is nothing—it has occurred to everybody; so has every thought that is worth fame. The expression of it is the thing to applaud. . . . Shakespeare took other people's quartz and extracted gold from it—it was a nearly valueless commodity before.

Marginal note

When the Lord finished the world, he pronounced it good. That is what I said about my first work, too. But Time, I tell you, Time takes the confidence out of these incautious early opinions. It is more than likely that He thinks about the world, now, pretty much as I think about the *Innocents Abroad*. The fact is, there is a trifle too much water in both.

Letter (November 6, 1886)

I wish I could give those sharp satires on European life which you mention, but of course a man can't write successful satire except he be in a calm, judicial good-humor; whereas I *hate* travel, and I *hate* hotels, and I *hate* the opera, and I *hate* the old masters. In truth, I don't ever seem to be in a good-enough humor with anything to satirize it. No, I want to stand up before it and curse it and foam at the mouth, or take a club and pound it to rags and pulp. I have got in two or three chapters about Wagner's operas, and managed to do it without showing temper, but the strain of another such effort would burst me!

Letter (November 1878)

. . . the man who does most toward deciding me as to whether I shall publish the book or burn it, is the man who always goes to sleep. If he drops off within fifteen minutes, I burn the book; if he keeps awake three-quarters of an hour, I publish—and I publish with the greatest confidence, too. For the intent of my works is to entertain; and by making this man comfortable on a sofa and timing him, I can tell within a shade or two what degree of success I am going to achieve. His verdict has burned several books for me—five, to be accurate.

"Whenever I Am about to Publish a Book" (1881–1885)

There has never been a time in the past thirty-five years when my literary shipyard didn't have two or more half-finished ships on the ways, neglected and baking in the sun; generally there have been three or four; at present there are five. This has an unbusiness-like look but it was not purposeless, it was intentional. As long as a book would write itself I was a faithful and interested amanuensis and my industry did not flag, but the minute that the book tried to shift to *my* head the labor of contriving its situations, inventing its adventures and conducting its conversations, I put it away and dropped it out of my mind. Then I examined my unfinished properties to see if among them there might not be one whose interest in itself had revived through a couple of years' restful idleness and was ready to take me on again as amanuensis.

Autobiography (August 30, 1906)

Words realize nothing, vivify nothing to you, unless you have suffered in your own person the thing which the words try to describe.

A Connecticut Yankee in King Arthur's Court (1889)

The mere knowledge of a fact is pale; but when you come to *realize* your fact, it takes on color. It is all the difference between hearing of a man being stabbed to the heart, and seeing it done.

A Connecticut Yankee in King Arthur's Court (1889)

If you wish to inflict a heartless and malignant punishment upon a young person, pledge him to keep a journal a year.

The Innocents Abroad (1869)

It reminds me of the journal I opened with the New Year, once, when I was a boy and a confiding and a willing prey to those impossible schemes of reform which well-meaning old maids and grandmothers set for the feet of unwary youths at that season of the year—setting oversized tasks for them, which, necessarily failing, as infallibly weaken the boy's strength of will, diminish his confidence in himself, and injure his chances of success in life. Please accept of an extract:

Monday—Got up, washed, went to bed.

Tuesday—Got up, washed, went to bed.

Wednesday—Got up, washed, went to bed.

Thursday—Got up, washed, went to bed.

Friday—Got up, washed, went to bed.

Friday fortnight—Got up, washed, went to bed.

Following month—Got up, washed, went to bed.

I stopped, then, discouraged. Startling events appeared to be too rare, in my career, to render a diary necessary. I still reflect with pride, however, that even at that early age I washed when I got up.

The Innocents Abroad (1869)

I like *Joan of Arc* best of all my books and it is the best, I know it perfectly well. And besides, it furnished me seven times the pleasure afforded me by any of the others; twelve years of preparation and two years of writing. The others needed no preparation, and got none.

Mark Twain, a Biography, Albert Bigelow Paine (1912)

If I were to sell the reader a barrel of molasses, and he, instead of sweetening his substantial dinner with the same at judicious intervals, should eat the entire barrel at one sitting, and then abuse me for making him sick, I would say that he deserved to be made sick for not knowing any better how to utilize the blessings this world affords. And if I sell to the reader this volume of nonsense, and he, instead of seasoning his graver reading with a chapter of it now and then, when his mind demands such relaxation, unwisely overdoses himself with several chapters of it at a single sitting, he will deserve to be nauseated, and he will have nobody to blame but himself if he is.

Preface, "Mark Twain's *Sketches*" (1872)

If you invent two or three people and turn them loose in your manuscript, something is bound to happen to them—you can't help it; and then it will take you the rest of the book to get them out of the natural consequences of that occurrence, and so, first thing you know, there's your book all finished up and never cost you an idea.

Letter (October 5, 1889)

A successful book is not made of what is in it,
but what is left out of it.

Letter (May 1897)

What are the proper proportions of a maxim?
A minimum of sound to a maximum of sense.

"Pudd'nhead Wilson's New Calendar," *Following the Equator* (1897)

My interest in a book ceases with the printing of it.

Letter (January 5, 1874)

[*A Tramp Abroad*]: I call it a gossipy volume, and that is what it is. It talks about anything and everything, and always drops a subject the moment my interest in it begins to slacken. It is as discursive as a conversation; it has no more restraints or limitations than a fireside talk has. I have been drifting around on an idle, easy-going tramp— so to speak—for a year, stopping when I pleased, moving on when I got ready. My book has caught the complexion of the trip. In a word, it is a book written by one loafer for a brother loafer to read.

Interview, "Mark Twain Interviewed," *New York World* (May 11, 1879)

The most useful and interesting letters we get here from home are from children seven or eight years old . . . they tell all they know, and then stop.

"A Complaint from Correspondents" (1866)

When you get an exasperating letter, what happens? If you are young, you answer it promptly, instantly—and mail the thing you have written. At forty what do you do? By that time you have found that a letter written in a passion is a mistake in ninety-nine cases out of a hundred.

Mark Twain, a Biography, Albert Bigelow Paine (1912)

. . . I am going to write you . . . but not now, for I haven't anything
to do and I can't write letters except when I am rushed.

Article, "My Author's League with Mark Twain," Dorothy Quick (1938)

I never write *metropolis* for seven cents because I can
get the same price for *city*. I never write *policeman*
because I can get the same money for *cop*.

Speech, "Spelling and Pictures" (1906)

You have a singularly fine and aristocratic disrespect for
homely and unpretending English. Every time I use "go
back" you get out your polisher and slick it up to "return."

Letter to a British copyeditor (1900)

It is the will of God that we must have critics, and missionaries,
and Congressmen, and humorists, and we must bear the
burden. Meantime, I seem to have been drifting into criticism
myself. But that is nothing. At the worst, criticism is nothing
more than a crime, and I am not unused to that.

My Autobiography (1907)

Criticism is a queer thing. If I print, "She was stark naked" and then proceed to describe her person in detail, what critic would not howl? Who would venture to leave the book on a parlor table? But the artist does this and all ages gather around and look and talk and point.

Mark Twain's Notebooks and Journals (1879)

No man has an appreciation so various that his judgment is good upon all varieties of literary work.

My Father: Mark Twain, Clara Clemens (1931)

I am not acquainted with my own books but I know Kipling's—at any rate I know them better than I know anybody else's books. They never grow pale to me; they keep their color; they are always fresh.

Autobiography (August 13, 1906)

One's glimpses and confusions, as one reads Browning, remind me of looking through a telescope (the small sort which you must move with your hand, not clock-work). You toil across dark spaces which are (to *your* lens) empty; but every now and then a splendor of stars and suns bursts upon you and fills the whole field with flame.

Mark Twain, a Biography, Albert Bigelow Paine (1912)

Cooper's art has some defects. In one place in *Deerslayer*, and in the restricted space of two-thirds of a page, Cooper has scored 114 offenses against literary art out of a possible 115. It breaks the record.

"Fenimore Cooper's Literary Offenses" (1895)

The conversations in the Cooper books have a curious sound in our modern ears. To believe that such talk really ever came out of people's mouths would be to believe that there was a time when time was of no value to a person who thought he had something to say; when it was the custom to spread a two-minute remark out to ten; when a man's mouth was a rolling-mill, and busied itself all day long in turning four-foot pigs of thought into thirty-foot bars of conversational railroad iron by attenuation; when subjects were seldom faithfully stuck to, but the talk wandered all around and arrived nowhere; when conversations consisted mainly of irrelevancies, with here and there a relevancy, a relevancy with an embarrassed look, as not being able to explain how it got there.

"Fenimore Cooper's Literary Offenses" (1895)

. . . her effort is entitled to the praise which the country journalist conferred upon the Essex band after he had praised the whole Fourth of July celebration in detail, and had exhausted his stock of compliments. But he was obliged to lay something of the nature of a complimentary egg, and with a final heroic effort he brought forth this, "The Essex band done the best they could."

Mark Twain's Autobiography (1924)

To me [Poe's] prose is unreadable—like Jane Austen's. No, there is a difference. I could read his prose on a salary, but not Jane's.

Letter (January 18, 1909)

For years my pet aversion had been the cuckoo clock; now here I was, at last, right in the creature's home; so wherever I went that distressing "*hoo*'hoo! *hoo*'hoo! *hoo*'hoo!" was always in my ears. For a nervous man, this was a fine state of things. Some sounds are hatefuler than others, but no sound is quite so inane, and silly, and aggravating as the "*hoo*'hoo!" of a cuckoo clock, I think. I bought one, and am carrying it home to a certain person; for I have always said that if the opportunity ever happened, I would do that man an ill turn. What I meant was that I would break one of his legs, or something of that sort; but in Lucerne I instantly saw that I could impair his mind. That would be more lasting, and more satisfactory every way. So I bought a cuckoo clock; and if I ever get home with it, he is "my meat," as they say in the mines. I thought of another candidate—a book-reviewer whom I could name if I wanted to—but after thinking it over, I didn't buy him a clock. I couldn't injure his mind.

A Tramp Abroad (1880)

I love to hear myself talk, because I get so much
instruction and moral upheaval out of it,
but I lose the bulk of this joy when I charge for it.

Letter (February 1906)

I thought some of the things I said were rather fine.
But he merely looked around at me, at distant intervals,
something as I have seen a benignant old cat look around
to see which kitten was meddling with her tail.

Roughing It (1872)

But Jim was asleep. Tom looked kind of ashamed, because you know a person always feels bad when he is talking uncommon fine and thinks the other person is admiring, and that other person goes to sleep that way. Of course he oughtn't to go to sleep, because it's shabby; but the finer a person talks the certainter it is to make you sleep, and so when you come to look at it it ain't nobody's fault in particular; both of them's to blame.

Tom Sawyer Abroad (1894)

Noise proves nothing. Often a hen who has merely laid an egg cackles as if she has laid an asteroid.

Following the Equator: A Journey Around the World (1897)

His voice was the effortless deep bass of a church organ, and would disturb the tranquility of a gas flame fifty yards away.

The American Claimant (1892)

It is eight or nine years since I bade good-bye to the lecture platform forever. But they say lecturers and burglars never reform. I don't know how it is with burglars—it is so long since I had intimate relations with those people—but it is quite true of lecturers. They never reform. Lecturers and readers say they are going to leave the lecture platform never to return. They mean it, they mean it. But there comes in time an overpowering temptation to come out on the platform and give truth and morality one more lift. You can't resist it.

Interview, "Mark Twain," *Pittsburgh Post* (December 29, 1884)

What a talker he is. He could persuade a fish to come out and take a walk with him.

Mark Twain's Notebook

It is my heart-warm and world-embracing Christmas hope and aspiration that all of us, the high, the low, the rich, the poor, the admired, the despised, the loved, the hated, the civilized, the savage (every man and brother of us all throughout the whole earth), may eventually be gathered together in a heaven of everlasting rest and peace and bliss, except the inventor of the telephone.

Gramophone recording (1890)

. . . for all the brag you hear about knowledge being such a wonderful thing, instink is worth forty of it for real unerringness.

Tom Sawyer Abroad (1894)

Learnin' by expe'ence. . . . There's a lot of such things, and *they* educate a person. . . . Uncle Abner said that the person that had took a bull by the tail once had learnt sixty or seventy times as much as a person that hadn't, and said a person that started in to carry a cat home by the tail was gitting knowledge that was always going to be useful to him, and warn't ever going to grow dim or doubtful.

Tom Sawyer Abroad (1894)

Jim said he'd bet it was a lesson to him.
"Yes," Tom says, "and like a considerable many lessons a body gets. They ain't no account, because the thing don't ever happen the same way again—and can't. The time Hen Scovil fell down the chimney and crippled his back for life, everybody said it would be a lesson to him. What kind of a lesson? How was he going to use it? He couldn't climb chimblies no more, and he hadn't no more backs to break."

Tom Sawyer Abroad (1894)

MARK TWAIN

It is noble to teach oneself; it is still nobler to teach others—
and less trouble.

Speech, "Introducing Doctor Van Dyke" (1923)

For seventy-two years I have been striving to
acquire that higher education which stands for
modesty and diffidence, and it doesn't work.

Speech, "Dedication Speech" (May 14, 1908)

Education consists mainly in what we have unlearned.

Mark Twain's Notebook

When I was a boy on the Mississippi River there was a
proposition in a township there to discontinue public schools
because they were too expensive. An old farmer spoke up and
said if they stopped the schools they would not save anything,
because every time a school was closed a jail had to be built.

Speech, "Public School Association" (November 23, 1900)

MONEY AND WORK

Simple rules for saving money: To save half, when
you are fired by an eager impulse to contribute to a
charity, wait, and count forty. To save three-quarters,
count sixty. To save it all, count sixty-five.

Following the Equator: A Journey Around the World (1897)

The lack of money is the root of all evil.
More Maxims of Mark, Merle Johnson (1927)

There are two times in a man's life when he should not
speculate: when he can't afford it, and when he can.
Following the Equator: A Journey Around the World (1897)

I remember . . . in the Hartford church the collection was being
taken up. The appeal had so stirred me that I could hardly wait for
the hat or plate to come my way. I had four hundred dollars in my
pocket, and I was anxious to drop it in the plate to come my way. I
had four hundred dollars in my pocket, and I was anxious to drop it
in the plate and wanted to borrow more. But the plate was so long
in coming my way that the fever-heat of beneficence was going
down lower and lower—going down at the rate of a hundred dollars
a minute. The plate was passed too late. When it finally came to
me, my enthusiasm had gone down so much that I kept my four
hundred dollars—and stole a dime from the plate. So, you see, time
sometimes leads to crime.

Oh, many a time have I thought of that and regretted it, and I
adjure you all to give while the fever is on you.

Speech, "Votes for Women" (January 20, 1901)

I see around me captains of all the illustrious industries,
most distinguished men; there are more than fifty here,
and I believe I know thirty-nine of them well. I could
probably borrow money from—from the others, anyway.

Speech, "Sixty-Seventh Birthday" (November 28, 1902)

Let your secret sympathies and your compassion be always
with the under dog in the fight—this is magnanimity,
but bet on the other one—this is business.

Mark Twain, a Biography, Albert Bigelow Paine (1912)

October. This is one of the peculiarly dangerous months to
speculate in stocks in. The others are July, January, September, April,
November, May, March, June, December, August and February.

"Pudd'nhead Wilson's Calendar,"
The Tragedy of Pudd'nhead Wilson (1894)

Unexpected money is a delight. The same sum
is a bitterness when you expected more.

Letter (March 23, 1878)

A banker is a person who lends you his umbrella when the
sun is shining and wants it back the minute it rains.

(Attributed)

The low level which commercial morality has reached in America
is deplorable. We have humble God-fearing Christian men
among us who will stoop to do things for a million dollars that
they ought not to be willing to do for less than two millions.

More Maxims of Mark, Merle Johnson (1927)

Him? Grasping? Insatiable? That man wouldn't be satisfied
if he had the contract to furnish hell with fuel.

Mark Twain's Notebooks and Journals (March 1886-June 1887)

I do not like work even when another person does it.

Europe and Elsewhere (1923)

I have often noticed that you shun exertion. There comes the difference between us. I court exertion. I love work. Why, sir, when I have a piece of work to perform, I go away to myself, sit down in the shade and muse over the coming enjoyment.

Letter (July 6, 1859)

Tom said to himself that it was not such a hollow world, after all. He had discovered a great law of human action, without knowing it—namely, that in order to make a man or a boy covet a thing, it is only necessary to make the thing difficult to attain. If he had been a great and wise philosopher, like the writer of this book, he would now have comprehended that Work consists of whatever a body is *obliged* to do, and that Play consists of whatever a body is not obliged to do. And this would help him to understand why constructing artificial flowers or performing on a treadmill is work while rolling ten-pins or climbing Mont Blanc is only amusement.

The Adventures of Tom Sawyer (1876)

Every man must learn his trade—not pick it up. God requires that he learn it by slow and painful processes. The apprentice-hand, in blacksmithing, in medicine, in literature, in everything, is a thing that can't be hidden. It always shows.

Letter to his brother Orion (March 23, 1878)

"Look here; there's one thing in this world which isn't ever cheap. That's a coffin. . . . There's one thing in this world which a person doesn't say, 'I'll look around a little, and if I find I can't do better, I'll come back and take it.' That's a coffin. There's one thing in this world which a person won't take in pine if he can go walnut; and won't take it in walnut if he can go mahogany; and won't take in mahogany if he can go an iron casket, with silver door-plate and bronze handles. That's a coffin. And there's one thing in this world which you don't have to worry around after a person to get him to pay for. And *that's* a coffin. Undertaking?—why it's the dead-surest business in Christendom, and the nobbiest."

Life on the Mississippi (1883)

MARK TWAIN

All things change except barbers, the ways of barbers, and the surroundings of barbers. These never change. What one experiences in a barber's shop the first time he enters is what he always experiences in barbers' shops afterward till the end of his days.

"About Barbers" (1871)

When we were finishing our house, we found we had a little cash left over, on account of the plumber not knowing it.

"The McWilliamses and the Burglar Alarm" (1882)

Your true pilot cares nothing about anything on earth but the river, and his pride in his occupation surpasses the pride of kings.

Life on the Mississippi (1883)

I do not know what to write, my life is so uneventful. I wish I was back there piloting up and down the river again. Verily, all is vanity and little worth—save piloting.

Letter to his mother and sister (January 20, 1866)

Certainly there is no nobler field for human effort than the insurance line of business—especially accident insurance. Ever since I have been a director of an accident-insurance company I have felt that I am a better man. Life has seemed more precious. Accidents have assumed a kindlier aspect. Distressing special providences have lost half their horror. I look upon a cripple now with affectionate interest—as an advertisement. I do not seem to care for poetry any more. I do not care for politics—even agriculture does not excite me. But to me now there is a charm about a railway collision that is unspeakable.

Speech, "Accident Insurance—Etc." (date unknown)

I would take charge of the constellations if I were asked to do it. All you need in this life is ignorance and confidence; then success is sure.

When Huck Finn Went Highbrow, Benjamin Casseres (1934)

You ought never to edit except when awake.

Letter to his editor (1900)

My days are given up to cursings—both loud and deep—
for I am reading the *Huckleberry Finn* proofs. They don't
make a very great many mistakes; but those that do occur
are of a nature to make a man curse his teeth loose.

Letter (1884)

Mr. Hall [publisher] wrote that the printer's proofreader
was improving my punctuation for me, and I telegraphed
orders to have him shot without giving him time to pray.

Letter (1889)

Your proofreader is an idiot; not only an idiot, but blind,
and not only blind, but partly dead. . . . He is blind and
dead and rotten, and ought to be thrown into the sewer.

Mark Twain's Notebook

I have always been able to gain my living without doing any work;
for the writing of books and magazine matter was always play,
not work. I enjoyed it; it was merely billiards to me.

Autobiography

Intellectual "work" is misnamed; it is a pleasure, a dissipation, and is its own highest reward. The poorest paid architect, engineer, general, author, sculptor, painter, lecturer, advocate, legislator, actor, preacher, singer is constructively in heaven when he is at work; and as for the musician with the fiddle-bow in his hand who sits in the midst of a great orchestra with the ebbing and flowing tides of divine sound washing over him—why, certainly, he is at work, if you wish to call it that, but lord, it's a sarcasm just the same. The law of work does seem utterly unfair—but there it is, and nothing can change it: the higher the pay in enjoyment the worker gets out of it, the higher shall be his pay in cash, also.

A Connecticut Yankee in King Arthur's Court (1889)

There are wise people who talk ever so knowingly and complacently about "the working classes," and satisfy themselves that a day's hard intellectual work is very much harder than a day's hard manual toil, and is righteously entitled to much bigger pay. But I know all about both; and so far as I'm concerned, there isn't money enough in the universe to hire me to swing a pickax thirty days, but I will do the hardest kind of intellectual work for just as near nothing as you can cipher it down.

A Connecticut Yankee in King Arthur's Court (1889)

Ladies and gentlemen, if any should ask, Why is it that you are here as introducer of the lecturer? I should answer that I happened to be around and was asked to perform this function. I was quite willing to do so, and, as there was no sort of need of an introduction, anyway, it could be necessary only that some person come forward for a moment and do an unnecessary thing, and this is quite in my line.

Speech, "Henry M. Stanley" (November 1886)

Do not put off till tomorrow what can be put off till day-after-tomorrow just as well.

More Maxims of Mark, Merle Johnson (1927)

Nature and Health

Thunder is good, thunder is impressive;
but it is lightning that does the work.

Letter (August 28, 1908)

I once heard a grouty Northern invalid say that a
coconut tree might be poetical, possibly it was;
but it looked like a feather-duster struck by lightning.

Roughing It (1872)

There is nothing like surface-mining to snatch the
graces and beauties and benignities out of a paradise,
and make an odious and repulsive spectacle of it.

Following the Equator: A Journey Around the World (1897)

Nothing is made in vain, but the fly came near it.

More Maxims of Mark, Merle Johnson (1927)

It is just like a man's vanity and impertinence to call an
animal dumb because it is dumb to his dull perceptions.

"What Is Man?" (1917)

The Bird of Birds—the Indian crow. I came to know him well, by and by, and be infatuated with him. I suppose he is the hardest lot that wears feathers. . . .

. . . this Indian sham-Quaker is just a rowdy, and is always noisy when awake—always chaffing, scolding, scoffing, laughing, ripping, and cursing, and carrying on about something or other. I never saw such a bird for delivering opinions. Nothing escapes him; he notices everything that happens, and brings out his opinion about it, particularly if it is a matter that is none of his business. And it is never a mild opinion, but always violent—violent and profane—the presence of ladies does not affect him. His opinions are not the outcome of reflection, for he never thinks about anything, but heaves out the opinion that is on top of his mind, and which is often an opinion about some quite different thing and does not fit the case. But that is his way; his main idea is to get out an opinion, and if he stopped to think he would lose chances.

Following the Equator: A Journey Around the World (1897)

You may call a jay a bird. Well, so he is, in a measure—because he's got feathers on him, and don't belong to no church, perhaps; but otherwise he is just as much a human as you be. And I'll tell you for why. A jay's gifts and instincts and feelings and interests cover the whole ground. A jay hasn't got any more principle than a Congressman. A jay will lie, a jay will steal, a jay will deceive, a jay will betray; and four times out of five, a jay will go back on his solemnest promise. The sacredness of an obligation is a thing which you can't cram into no blue-jay's head. Now on top of all this, there's another thing: a jay can out-swear any gentleman in the mines.

A Tramp Abroad (1880)

The magpie was out in great force, in the fields and on the fences. He is a handsome large creature, with snowy white decorations, and is a singer; he has a murmurous rich note that is lovely. He was once modest, even diffident; but he lost all that when he found out that he was Australia's sole musical bird. He has talent, and cuteness, and impudence; and in his tame state he is a most satisfactory pet—never coming when he is called, always coming when he isn't, and studying disobedience as an accomplishment. He is not confined, but loafs all over the house and grounds, like the laughing jackass. I think he learns to talk, I know he learns to sing tunes, and his friends say that he knows how to steal without learning.

Following the Equator: A Journey Around the World (1897)

Many a time, when I have seen a man abusing a horse, I have wished
I knew that horse's language, so that I could whisper in his ear,
"Fool, you are master here, if you but knew it. Launch out with your
heels!" The working millions, in all the ages, have been horses.

"The New Dynasty" (1886)

. . . I am not an expert in horses and do not speak with assurance.
I can always tell which is the front end of a horse,
but beyond that my art is not above the ordinary.

Mark Twain, a Biography, Albert Bigelow Paine (1912)

The urbane livery-stable keeper furnished me with a solemn,
short-bodied, long-legged animal—a sort of animated counting-
house stool, as it were—which he called a "Morgan" horse.
He told me who the brute was "sired" by, and was proceeding to
tell me who he was "dammed" by but I gave him to understand
that I was competent to damn the horse myself . . .

"The Great Prize Fight," *The Golden Era* (October 11, 1863)

Sagebrush is a very fair fuel, but as a vegetable it is a distinguished failure. Nothing can abide the taste of it but the jackass and his illegitimate child the mule. But their testimony to its nutriousness is worth nothing, for they will eat pine knots or anthracite coal, or brass filings, or lead pipe, or old bottles, or anything that comes handy, and then go off looking as grateful as if they had had oysters for dinner. Mules and donkeys and camels have appetites that anything will relieve temporarily, but nothing satisfy.

Roughing It (1872)

There warn't anybody at the church, except maybe a hog or two, for there warn't any lock on the door, and hogs like a puncheon floor in summer-time because it's cool. If you notice, most folks don't go to church only when they've got to; but a hog is different.

Adventures of Huckleberry Finn (1884)

The cayote is a long, slim, sick and sorry-looking skeleton, with a gray wolf-skin stretched over it, a tolerably bushy tail that forever sags down with a despairing expression of forsakenness and misery, a furtive and evil eye, and a long, sharp face, with slightly lifted lip and exposed teeth. He has a general slinking expression all over. The cayote is a living, breathing allegory of Want. He is *always* hungry. He is always poor, out of luck and friendless. The meanest creatures despise him, and even the fleas would desert him for a velocipede. He is so spiritless and cowardly that even while his exposed teeth are pretending a threat, the rest of his face is apologizing for it. And he is *so* homely!—so scrawny and ribby and coarse-haired and pitiful. When he sees you he lifts his lip and lets a flash of his teeth out, and then turns a little out of the course he was pursuing, depresses his head a bit, and strikes a long, soft-footed trot through the sagebrush, glancing over his shoulder at you, from time to time, till he is about out of easy pistol range, and then he stops and takes a deliberate survey of you; he will trot fifty yards and stop again— another fifty and stop again; and finally the gray of his gliding body blends with the gray of the sagebrush and he disappears.

Roughing It (1872)

If you pick up a starving dog and make him prosperous, he will not bite you. This is the principal difference between a dog and a man.

The Tragedy of Pudd'nhead Wilson (1894)

By what right has the dog come to be regarded as a "noble" animal? The more brutal and cruel and unjust you are to him the more your fawning and adoring slave he becomes; whereas, if you shamefully misuse a cat once she will always maintain a dignified reserve toward you afterward—you can never get her full confidence.

Mark Twain, a Biography, Albert Bigelow Paine (1912)

Before the shearing the sheep looked like the fat woman in the circus; after it he looked like a bench.

Following the Equator: A Journey Around the World (1897)

The porpoise is the clown of the sea—evidently does his wild antics for pure fun; there is no sordid profit in it.

Mark Twain's Notebook

There are narrow escapes in India. In the very jungle where I killed 16 tigers and all those elephants, a cobra bit me, but it got well; everyone was surprised. This could not happen twice in ten years, perhaps. Usually death would result in fifteen minutes.

Following the Equator: A Journey Around the World (1897)

There in the Black Forest, on the mountainside, I saw an ant go through such a performance as this with a dead spider of fully ten times his own weight. The spider was not quite dead, but too far gone to resist. He had a round body the size of a pea. The little ant—observing that I was noticing—turned him on his back, sunk his fangs into his throat, lifted him into the air and started vigorously off with him, stumbling over little pebbles, stepping on the spider's legs and tripping himself up, dragging him backward, shoving him bodily ahead, dragging him up stones six inches high instead of going around them, climbing weeds twenty times his own height and jumping from their summits—and finally leaving him in the middle of the road to be confiscated by any other fool of an ant that wanted him. I measured the ground which this ass traversed, and arrived at the conclusion that what he had accomplished inside of twenty minutes would constitute some such job as this—relatively speaking—for a man; to wit: to strap two eight-hundred-pound horses together, carry them eighteen hundred feet, mainly over (not around) boulders averaging six feet high, and in the course of the journey climb up and jump from the top of one precipice like Niagara, and three steeples, each a hundred and twenty feet high; and then put the horses down, in an exposed place, without anybody to watch them, and go off to indulge in some other idiotic miracle for vanity's sake.

A Tramp Abroad (1880)

Science has recently discovered that the ant does not lay up anything for winter use. This will knock him out of literature, to some extent. He does not work, except when people are looking, and only then when the observer has a green, naturalistic look and seems to be taking notes. This amounts to deception, and will injure him for the Sunday schools. He has not judgment enough to know what is good to eat from what isn't. This amounts to ignorance and will impair the world's respect for him. He cannot stroll around a stump and find his way home again. This amounts to idiocy, and once the damaging fact is established, thoughtful people will cease to look up to him, the sentimental will cease to fondle him. His vaunted industry is but a vanity and of no effect, since he never gets home with anything he starts with. This disposes of the last remnant of his reputation and wholly destroys his main usefulness as a moral agent, since it will make the sluggard hesitate to go to him any more. It is strange beyond comprehension that

MARK TWAIN

so manifest a humbug as the ant has been able to fool so many nations and keep it up so many ages without being found out.

A Tramp Abroad (1880)

. . . we had quite a menagerie [of tarantulas] arranged along the shelves of the room. Some of these spiders could straddle over a common saucer with their hairy, muscular legs, and when their feelings were hurt, or their dignity offended, they were the wickedest-looking desperadoes the animal world can furnish. If their glass prison-houses were touched ever so lightly they were up and spoiling for a fight in a minute. Starchy?—proud? Indeed, they would take up a straw and pick their teeth like a member of Congress.

Roughing It (1872)

[In Honolulu]: Mosquitoes, two kinds—day and night.

Mark Twain's Notebook

Courage is resistance to fear, mastery of fear—not absence of fear. Except a creature be part coward, it is not a compliment to say it is brave; it is merely a loose misapplication of the word. Consider the flea!—incomparably the bravest of all the creatures of God, if ignorance of fear were courage. Whether you are asleep or awake he will attack you, caring nothing for the fact that in bulk and strength you are to him as are the massed armies of the earth to a sucking child; he lives both day and night and all days and nights in the very lap of peril and the immediate presence of death and yet is no more afraid than is the man who walks the streets of a city that was threatened by an earthquake ten centuries before. When we speak of Clive, Nelson, and Putnam as men who "didn't know what fear was," we ought always to add the flea—and put him at the head of the procession.

"Pudd'nhead Wilson's Calendar,"
The Tragedy of Pudd'nhead Wilson (1894)

Not one of us could have planned the fly, not one of us could have constructed him; and no one would have considered it wise to try, except under an assumed name.

"Thoughts of God" (early 1900s)

Man seems to be a rickety poor sort of a thing, any way you take him; a kind of British Museum of infirmities and inferiorities. He is always undergoing repairs. A machine that was as unreliable as he is would have no market.

Letters from the Earth (1962)

He had had much experience of physicians, and said, "The only way to keep your health is to eat what you don't want, drink what you don't like, and do what you'd druther not."

"Pudd'nhead Wilson's New Calendar," *Following the Equator* (1897)

Doctors do know so little and they do charge so much for it.

Letter (August 12, 1908)

[Before being operated upon]: Console yourself with the reflection that you are giving the doctor pleasure, and that he is getting paid for it.

Mark Twain, Archibald Henderson (1912)

[He] went swaggering around in his bandages showing off like an innocent big child . . . He was prouder of being wounded than a really modest person would be of being killed.

Personal Recollections of Joan of Arc (1896)

I have never taken any exercise, except sleeping and resting, and I never intend to take any. Exercise is loathsome. And it cannot be any benefit when you are tired; and I was always tired. But let another person try my way, and see where he will come out.

Speech, "Seventieth Birthday" (December 5, 1905)

There would be a power of fun in skating if you could do it with somebody else's muscles.

Letter (December 18, 1874)

I tell you skating is an accomplishment suited only to youth and comeliness of face and symmetry. . . . But you . . . when you are on skates you waddle off as stuffy and stupid and ungainly as a buzzard that's had half a horse for dinner.

Interview, *Morning Chronicle* (February 22, 1869)

Get a bicycle. You will not regret it. If you live.

"Taming the Bicycle" (1917)

The game of billiards has destroyed my naturally sweet disposition. Once, when I was an underpaid reporter in Virginia City, whenever I wished to play billiards I went out to look for an easy mark. One day a stranger came to town and opened a billiard parlor. I looked him over casually. When he proposed a game, I answered, "All right."

"Just knock the balls around a little so that I can get your gait," he said; and when I had done so, he remarked: "I will be perfectly fair with you. I'll play you left-handed." I felt hurt, for he was cross-eyed, freckled, and had red hair, and I determined to teach him a lesson. He won first shot, ran out, took my half-dollar, and all I got was the opportunity to chalk my cue.

"If you can play like that with your left hand," I said, "I'd like to see you play with your right."

"I can't," he said. "I'm left-handed."

Speech, "Billiards" (April 24, 1906)

I always take it [Scotch whiskey] at night as a
preventative of toothache. I have never had the toothache;
and what is more, I never intend to have it.

Europe and Elsewhere (1897)

Never smoke any Italian tobacco. Never do it on any account. It
makes me shudder to think what it must be made of. You cannot
throw an old cigar "stub" down anywhere, but some vagabond
will pounce upon it on the instant. I like to smoke a good deal,
but it wounds my sensibilities to see one of these stub-hunters
watching me out of the corners of his hungry eyes and calculating
how long my cigar will be likely to last. It reminded me too
painfully of that San Francisco undertaker who used to go to
sick beds with his watch in his hand and time the corpse.

The Innocents Abroad (1869)

I have made it a rule never to smoke more than one cigar at a
time. I have no other restriction as regards smoking. I do not
know just when I began to smoke, I only know that it was in my
father's lifetime, and that I was discreet. He passed from this life

MARK TWAIN

early in 1847, when I was a shade past eleven; ever since then I have smoked publicly. As an example to others, and not that I care for moderation myself, it has always been my rule never to smoke when asleep, and never to refrain when awake. It is a good rule. I mean, for me; but some of you know quite well that it wouldn't answer for everybody that's trying to get to be seventy.

Speech, "Seventieth Birthday" (December 5, 1905)

. . . when they used to tell me I'd shorten my life ten years by smoking, they little knew the devotee they were wasting their puerile words upon—they little knew how trivial and valueless I would regard a decade that had no smoking in it!

Letter (December 19, 1870)

This memory of ours stores up a perfect record of the most useless facts and anecdotes and experiences. And all the things that we ought to know—that we need to know—that we'd profit by knowing—it casts aside with the careless indifference of a girl refusing her true lover.

Speech, "Morals and Memory" (date unknown)

He had a good memory, and a tongue hung in the middle. This is a combination which gives immortality to conversation.

Roughing It (1872)

For many years I believed that I remembered helping my grandfather drink his whiskey toddy when I was six weeks old, but I do not tell about that any more, now; I am grown old, and my memory is not as active as it used to be. When I was younger I could remember anything, whether it had happened or not; but my faculties are decaying, now, and soon I shall be so I cannot remember any but the things that happened. It is sad to go to pieces like this, but we all have to do it.

My Autobiography (1907)

I was always heedless. I was heedless; and therefore I was constantly, and quite unconsciously, committing breaches of the minor proprieties, which brought upon me humiliations which ought to have humiliated me but didn't, because I didn't know anything had happened.

My Autobiography (1907)

The proverb says, "Born lucky, *always* lucky," and I am very superstitious. As a small boy I was notoriously lucky. It was usual for one or two of our lads (per annum) to get drowned in the Mississippi or in Bear Creek, but I was pulled out in a 2/3 drowned condition 9 times before I learned to swim, and was considered to be a cat in disguise. When the "Pennsylvania" blew up and the telegraph reported my brother as fatally injured (with 60 others) but made no mention of me, my uncle said to my mother, "It means that Sam was somewhere else, after being on that boat a year and a half—he was born lucky." Yes, I *was* somewhere else. I am so superstitious that I have always been afraid to have business dealings with certain relatives and friends of mine because they were unlucky people. All my life I have stumbled upon lucky chances of large size, and whenever they were wasted it was because of my own stupidity and carelessness.

Letter (c. 1895)

For several years I have been intending to stop writing for print as soon as I could afford it. At last I can afford it, and have put the pot-boiler pen away. What I have been wanting is a chance to write a book without reserves—a book which should take account of no one's feelings, and no one's prejudices, opinions, beliefs, hopes, illusions, delusions; a book which should say my say, right out of my heart, in the plainest language and without a limitation of any sort. I judged that that would be an unimaginable luxury, heaven on earth.

Letter (May 12, 1899)

I have been dictating this autobiography of mine daily for three months; I have thought of fifteen hundred or two thousand incidents in my life which I am ashamed of, but I have not gotten one of them to consent to go on paper yet.

My Autobiography (1907)

I retired from work on my seventieth birthday. Since then I have been putting in merely twenty-six hours a day dictating my autobiography, which, as John Phoenix said in regard to his autograph, may be relied upon as authentic, as it is written exclusively by me. But it is not to be published in full until I am thoroughly dead. I have made it as caustic, fiendish, and devilish as possible. It will fill many volumes, and I shall continue writing it until the time comes for me to join the angels. It is going to be a terrible autobiography. It will make the hair of some folks curl. But it cannot be published until I am dead, and the persons mentioned in it and their children and grandchildren are dead. It is something awful!

Speech, "Dress Reform and Copyright" (1906)

An autobiography is the most treacherous thing there is. It lets out every secret the author is trying to keep; it lets the truth shine unobstructed through every harmless deception he tries to play. . . . I am speaking from autobiographical personal experience.

Autobiography

I came in with Halley's Comet in 1835. It is coming again next year [1910], and I expect to go out with it. It will be the greatest disappointment of my life if I don't go out with Halley's Comet. The Almighty has said, no doubt: "Now here are these two unaccountable freaks; they came in together, they must go out together."

Mark Twain, a Biography, Albert Bigelow Paine (1912)

Patriotism and Politics

My kind of loyalty was loyalty to one's country, not to its institutions or its office-holders. The country is the real thing, the substantial thing, the eternal thing; it is the thing to watch over, and care for, and be loyal to; institutions are extraneous, they are its mere clothing, and clothing can wear out.

A Connecticut Yankee in King Arthur's Court (1889)

Word it as softly as you please, the spirit of patriotism is the spirit of the dog and the wolf. The moment there is a misunderstanding about a boundary line or a hamper of fish or some other squalid matter, see patriotism rise, and hear him split the universe with his war-whoop. The spirit of patriotism being in its nature jealous and selfish, is just in man's line, it comes natural to him—he can live up to all its requirements to the letter; but the spirit of Christianity is not in its entirety possible to him.

Mark Twain's Notebook

Patriot: The person who can holler the loudest without knowing what he is hollering about.

More Maxims of Mark, Merle Johnson (1927)

It could probably be shown by facts and figures that there is no distinctly native American criminal class except Congress.

Following the Equator: A Journey Around the World (1897)

Suppose you were an idiot. And suppose you were
a member of Congress. But I repeat myself.

Mark Twain, a Biography, Albert Bigelow Paine (1912)

Whenever you find that you are on the side of the majority,
it is time to reform (or pause and reflect).

Mark Twain's Notebook

Hain't we got all the fools in town on our side?
And ain't that a big enough majority in any town?

The Adventures of Huckleberry Finn (1884)

An honest man in politics shines more than he would elsewhere.

A Tramp Abroad (1880)

St. Patrick had no politics; his sympathies lay with the right—
that was politics enough. When he came across a reptile,
he forgot to inquire whether he was a Democrat or a Republican,
but simply exalted his staff and "let him him have it."

"Letter Read at a Dinner of the Knights of St. Patrick" (March 16, 1876)

What, then, is the true Gospel of consistency? Change. Who is the
really consistent man? The man who changes. Since change is the
law of his being, he cannot be consistent if he stick in a rut.

"Consistency" (1884)

There is no man so poor but what at intervals some man comes to
him with an ax to grind. By and by the ax's aspect becomes familiar
to the proprietor of the grindstone. He perceives that it is the same
old ax. If you are a governor you know that the stranger wants an
office. The first time he arrives you are deceived; he pours out such
noble praises of you and your political record that you are moved to
tears; there's a lump in your throat and you are thankful that you have
lived for this happiness. Then the stranger discloses his ax, and you
are ashamed of yourself and your race. Six repetitions will cure you.

Mark Twain, a Biography, Albert Bigelow Paine (1912)

For fifty years our country has been a constitutional monarchy, with the Republican party sitting on the throne. . . . Ours is not only a monarchy but a hereditary monarchy—in the one political family. It passes from heir to heir as regularly and as surely and as unpreventably as does any throne in Europe.

Autobiography (July 16, 1908)

Mr. [Theodore] Roosevelt is the most formidable disaster that has befallen the country since the Civil War—but the vast mass of the nation loves him, is frantically fond of him, even idolizes him. This is the simple truth. It sounds like a libel upon the intelligence of the human race but it isn't; there isn't any way to libel the intelligence of the human race.

Autobiography (September 7, 1907)

In the South the war is what A.D. is elsewhere; they date from it.

Life on the Mississippi (1883)

The educated Southerner has no use for an *r*, except at the beginning of a word. He says "honah," and "dinnah," and "Gove'nuh," and "befo' the waw," and so on. The words may lack charm to the eye, in print, but they have it to the ear. When did the *r* disappear from Southern speech, and how did it come to disappear? The custom of dropping it was not borrowed from the North, nor inherited from England. Many Southerners— most Southerners—put a y into occasional words that begin with the k sound. For instance, they say Mr. K'yahtah (Carter) and speak of playing k'yahds or of riding in the k'yahs. And they have the pleasant custom—long ago fallen into decay in the North—of frequently employing the respectful "Sir." Instead of the curt *Yes*, and the abrupt *No*, they say "Yes, Suh," "No, Suh."

Life on the Mississippi (1883)

We asked a passenger who belonged there what sort of place [Arkansas] was. "Well," said he, after considering, and with the air of one who wishes to take time and be accurate, "It's a hell of a place." A description which was photographic for exactness.

Life on the Mississippi (1883)

Mississippi steamboating was born about 1812; at the end
of thirty years it had grown to mighty proportions; and in
less than thirty more it was dead. A strangely short life for so
majestic a creature. Of course it is not absolutely dead; neither
is a crippled octogenarian who could once jump twenty-two
feet on level ground; but as contrasted with what it was in its
prime vigor, Mississippi steamboating may be called dead.

Life on the Mississippi (1883)

For a tranquil pleasure excursion, there was nothing equal to a raft.

"Facts Concerning the Recent Resignation" (1903)

But seriously a Washoe wind is by no means a trifling matter.
It blows flimsy houses down, lifts shingle roofs occasionally, rolls up
tin ones like sheet music, now and then blows a stage coach over
and spills the passengers; and tradition says the reason there are
so many bald people there, is, that the wind blows the hair off
their heads while they are looking skyward after their hats.

Carson streets seldom look inactive on Summer afternoons, because there are so many citizens skipping around their escaping hats, like chambermaids trying to head off a spider.

Roughing It (1872)

. . . the Carson—a river, 20 yards wide, knee deep, and so villainously rapid and crooked that it looks like it had wandered into the country without intending it, and had run about in a bewildered way and got lost, in its hurry to get out again before some thirsty man came along and drank it up. I said we are situated in a flat, sandy desert—true. And surrounded on all sides by such prodigious mountains that when you gaze at them awhile—and begin to conceive of their grandeur—and next to feel their vastness expanding your soul—and ultimately find yourself growing and swelling and spreading into a giant—I say when this point is reached, you look disdainfully down upon the insignificant village of Carson, and in that instant you are seized with a burning desire to stretch forth your hand, put the city in your pocket, and walk off with it.

Letter to his mother (October 1861)

Fort Yuma is probably the hottest place on earth. The thermometer stays at one-hundred and twenty in the shade there all the time— except when it varies and goes higher. It is a U.S. military post, and its occupants get so used to the terrific heat that they suffer without it. There is a tradition . . . that a very, very wicked soldier died there, once, and of course went straight to the hottest corner of perdition,—and the next day he *telegraphed back for his blankets*.

Roughing It (1872)

Three months of camp life on Lake Tahoe would restore an Egyptian mummy to his pristine vigor, and give him an appetite like an alligator. I do not mean the oldest and driest mummies, of course, but the fresher ones. The air up there in the clouds is very pure and fine, bracing and delicious. And why shouldn't it be?—it is the same the angels breathe.

Roughing It (1872)

I reverently believe that the Maker who made us all makes everything in New England but the weather. I don't know who makes that, but I think it must be raw apprentices in the weather-clerk's factory who experiment and learn how, in New England, for board and clothes, and then are promoted to make weather for countries that require a good article, and will take their custom elsewhere if they don't get it. There is a sumptuous variety about the New England weather that compels the stranger's admiration—and regret. The weather is always doing something there; always attending strictly to business; always getting up new designs and trying them on the people to see how they will go.

Speech, "The Weather" (December 22, 1876)

I met [an old man] out in Iowa who had come up from Arkansas. I asked him whether he had experienced much cold during the preceding winter, and he exclaimed, "Cold! If the thermometer had been an inch longer we'd all have frozen to death!"

Mark Twain and I, Opie Read (1940)

I had to visit Niagara fifteen times before I succeeded in getting my imaginary Falls gauged to the actuality and could begin to sanely and wholesomely wonder at them for what they were, not what I had expected them to be. When I first approached them it was with my face lifted toward the sky, for I thought I was going to see an Atlantic Ocean pouring down thence, over cloud-vexed Himalayan heights, a sea-green wall of water sixty miles front and six miles high, and so, when the toy reality came suddenly into view—that beruffled little wet apron hanging out to dry—the shock was too much for me, and I fell with a dull thud.

Yet slowly, surely, steadily, in the course of my fifteen visits, the proportions adjusted themselves to the facts, and I came at last to realize that a waterfall a hundred and sixty-five feet high and a quarter of a mile wide was an impressive thing. It was not a dipperful to my vanished great vision, but it would answer.

Following the Equator: A Journey Around the World (1897)

I am most infernally tired of Washington and its "attractions." To be busy is a man's only happiness—and I am—otherwise I should die.

To his brother Orion (February 21, 1868)

We must judge of a city, as of a man, by its external appearances and by its inward character. In externals the foreigner coming to these shores is more impressed at first by our sky-scrapers. They are new to him. He has not done anything of the sort since he built the tower of Babel. The foreigner is shocked by them.

In the daylight they are ugly. They are—well, too chimneyfied and too snaggy—like a mouth that needs attention from a dentist; like a cemetery that is all monuments and no gravestones. But at night, seen from the river where they are columns towering against the sky, all sparkling with light, they are fairylike; they are beauty more satisfactory to the soul and more enchanting than anything that man has dreamed of since the Arabian nights. . . . When your foreigner makes disagreeable comments on New York by daylight, float him down the river at night.

Speech, "Municipal Government" (December 6, 1900)

I think that in the [African-American] Jubilees and their songs America has produced the perfectest flower of the ages; and I wish it were a foreign product, so that she would worship it and lavish money on it and go properly crazy over it.

Letter (August 22, 1897)

What a funny thing is monarchy. . . . It assumes that a wrong maintained for a dozen or a thousand years becomes a right. It assumes that the wronged parties will presently give up and take the same view. . . . Now, by an effort one can imagine a family of bears taking pride in the historic fact that an ancestor of theirs took violent possession of a bee tree some centuries ago, and that the family have had a right to it ever since . . . but here the allegory fails; for the bees would attack the bears every day for a thousand years. You can make a man understand how time turns a wrong into a right, but you can't make a bee understand—in his present undeveloped stage.

Mark Twain's Notebook

Scoffing democrats as we are, we do dearly love to be noticed by a duke, and when we are noticed by a monarch we have softening of the brain for the rest of our lives. We try our best to keep from referring to these precious collisions, and in time some of us succeed in keeping our dukes and monarchs to ourselves; it costs us something to do this but in time we accomplish it. In my own case, I have so carefully and persistently trained myself in this kind of self-denial that today I can look on calm and unmoved when a returned American is casually and gratefully playing the earls he has met: I can look on, silent and unexcited, and never offer to call his hand, although I have three kings and a pair of emperors up my sleeve.

Autobiography (December 2, 1907)

No throne exists that has a right to exist, and no symbol of it, flying from any flagstaff, is righteously entitled to wear any device but the skull and crossbones of that kindred industry which differs from royalty only businesswise—merely as retail differs from wholesale.

The American Claimant (1892)

I will say this much for the nobility: that, tyrannical, murderous, rapacious, and morally rotten as they were, they were deeply and enthusiastically religious.

A Connecticut Yankee in King Arthur's Court (1889)

A monarch, when good, is entitled to the consideration which we accord to a pirate who keeps Sunday school between crimes; when bad, he is entitled to none at all.

Mark Twain's Notebooks (c. 1888–1889)

RELIGIONS

I cannot see how a man of any large degree of humorous
perception can ever be religious—except he purposely
shut the eyes of his mind and keep them shut by force.

Mark Twain's Notebooks and Journals (c. 1879)

He is a marvel—man is! I wish I knew who invented him.

Letters from the Earth (1962)

There was never a century nor a country that was short of experts who knew the Deity's mind and were willing to reveal it.

"As Concerns Interpreting the Deity" (1905)

Temperate temperance is the best. Intemperate temperance injures the cause of temperance, while temperate temperance helps it in its fight against intemperate intemperance. Fanatics will never learn that, though it be written in letters of gold across the sky.

Mark Twain's Notebook

Reverence for one's own sacred things—parents, religion, flag, laws, and respect for one's own beliefs—these are feelings which we cannot even help. They come natural to us; they are involuntary, like breathing. There is no personal merit in breathing. But the reverence which is difficult, and which has personal merit in it, is the respect which you pay, without compulsion, to the political or religious attitude of a man whose beliefs are not yours. You can't revere his gods or his politics, and no one expects you to do that, but you could respect his belief in them if you tried hard enough; and you could respect *him*, too, if you tried enough. But it is very, very difficult; it is next to impossible, and so we hardly ever try. If the man doesn't believe as we do, we say he is a crank, and that settles it. I mean it does nowadays, because we can't burn them.

Following the Equator: A Journey Around the World (1897)

India has two million gods, and worships them all. In religion all other countries are paupers; India is the only millionaire.

Following the Equator: A Journey Around the World (1897)

The so-called Christian nations are the most enlightened and progressive . . . but in spite of their religion, not because of it. The Church has opposed every innovation and discovery from the day of Galileo down to our own time, when the use of anesthetics in childbirth was regarded as a sin because it avoided the biblical curse pronounced against Eve. And every step in astronomy and geology ever taken has been opposed by bigotry and superstition. The Greeks surpassed us in artistic culture and in architecture five hundred years before the Christian religion was born.

Mark Twain, a Biography, Albert Bigelow Paine (1912)

Who prays for Satan? Who, in eighteen centuries, has had the common humanity to pray for the one sinner that needed it most?

The Autobiography of Mark Twain (1959)

One of [the Maoris of New Zealand] thought the missionary had got everything wrong end first and upside down. "Why, he wants us to stop worshiping and supplicating the evil gods, and go to worshiping and supplicating the Good One! There is no sense in that. A *good* god is not going to do us any harm."

Following the Equator: A Journey Around the World (1897)

When a thing is sacred to me it is impossible for me to be irreverent toward it. I cannot call to mind a single instance where I have ever been irreverent, except towards the things which were sacred to other people.

"Is Shakespeare Dead?" (1909)

Often, the less there is to justify a traditional custom, the harder it is to get rid of it.

The Adventures of Tom Sawyer (1876)

Man . . . is kind enough when he is not excited by religion.

"A Horse's Tale" (1906)

[The preacher] never charged nothing for his preaching, and it was worth it, too.

Adventures of Huckleberry Finn (1884)

True irreverence is disrespect for another man's god.

"Pudd'nhead Wilson's New Calendar," *Following the Equator* (1897)

[Satan]: "It is true, that which I have revealed to you; there is no God, no universe, no human race, no earthly life, no heaven, no hell. It is all a dream—a grotesque and foolish dream. Nothing exists but you. And you are but a thought—a vagrant thought, a useless thought, a homeless thought, wandering forlorn among the empty eternities!"

He vanished, and left me appalled; for I knew, and realized, that all he had said was true.

"The Mysterious Stranger" (1916)

All men have heard of the Mormon Bible, but few except the "elect" have seen it, or, at least, taken the trouble to read it. I brought away a copy from Salt Lake. The book is a curiosity to me, it is such a pretentious affair, and yet so "slow," so sleepy; such an insipid mess of inspiration. It is chloroform in print.

Roughing It (1872)

Religion consists in a set of things which the average man thinks he believes and wishes he was certain.

Notebook (1879)

[The Bible] has noble poetry in it; and some clever fables;
and some blood drenched history; and a wealth of obscenity;
and upwards of a thousand lies.

Letters from the Earth (1862)

In five or six thousand years five or six high civilizations have
risen, flourished, commanded the wonder of the world, then faded
out and disappeared; and not one of them except the latest ever
invented any sweeping and adequate way to kill people. They all
did their best—to kill being the chiefest ambition of the human
race and the earliest incident in its history—but only the Christian
civilization has scored a triumph to be proud of. Two or three
centuries from now it will be recognized that all the competent
killers are Christians; then the pagan world will go to school
to the Christian—not to acquire his religion, but his guns.

"The Mysterious Stranger" (1916)

Bibliography and Works Cited

Selected works published by Mark Twain in his lifetime:

Adventures of Huckleberry Finn. 1884 (first publication in America, 1885).
The Adventures of Tom Sawyer. 1876.
A Connecticut Yankee in King Arthur's Court. 1889.
Following the Equator: A Journey Around the World. 1897.
The Gilded Age: A Tale of To-Day. (with Charles Dudley Warner.) 1873.
Innocents Abroad. 1889.
Life on the Mississippi. 1883.
The Prince and the Pauper. 1882.
Roughing It. 1872.
Sketches New and Old. 1875.
The $30,000 Bequest and Other Stories. 1872.
Those Extraordinary Twins. 1894.
Tom Sawyer Abroad. 1894.
Tom Sawyer, Detective. 1896.
The Tragedy of Pudd'nhead Wilson. 1894.
A Tramp Abroad. 1880.

*Collections of posthumous works and recollections or compilations
by friends, family, acquaintances, and editors:*

The Autobiography of Mark Twain. Charles Neider. New York: Harper, 1959.

Bite-Size Twain: Wit and Wisdom from the Literary Legend. Compiled by John P. Holms and Karin Baji. New York: St. Martin's Press, 1998.

The Comic Mark Twain Reader: The Most Humorous Selections from His Stories, Sketches, Novels, Travel Books, and Speeches. Edited by Charles Neider. Garden City, New York: Doubleday and Company, 1977.

The Devil's Race-Track: Mark Twain's Great Dark Writings (The Best from *Which Was the Dream?* and *Fables of Man*). Edited by John S. Tuckey. Berkeley: University of California Press, 1980.

The Diaries of Adam and Eve and Other Stories. Mineola, New York: Dover, 2008.

Humorous Stories and Sketches. Edited by Philip Smith. Mineola, New York: Dover, 1996.

The Complete Letters of Mark Twain. Middlesex, England: Echo Library, 2007.

Mark My Words: Mark Twain on Writing. Edited by Mark Dawidziak. New York: St. Martin's Press, 1996.

Mark Twain, a Biography. Albert Bigelow Paine. New York: Harper and Brothers, 1912.

Mark Twain at Your Fingertips: A Book of Quotations. Compiled and edited by Caroline Thomas Harnsberger. Mineola, New York: Dover, 2009.

Mark Twain in Eruption: Hitherto Unpublished Pages about Men and Events. Edited by Bernard DeVoto. New York: Capricorn Books, 1968.

Mark Twain Laughing: Humorous Anecdotes by and about Samuel L. Clemens. Paul M. Zall. Knoxville: University of Tennessee Press, 1987.

Mark Twain on Man and Beast. Janet Smith. New York: Lawrence Hill and Company, 1972.

Mark Twain's Letters. Edited by Albert Bigelow Paine. New York: Harper and Brothers, 1917.

Mark Twain's Notebook. Edited by Albert Bigelow Paine. New York: Harper and Brothers, 1935.

Mark Twain's Notebooks & Journals. Volume I (1855–1873) and Volume II (1877–1883). The Mark Twain Papers. Berkeley: University of California Press, 1976.

Mark Twain Speaking. Paul Fatout. Iowa City: University of Iowa Press, 1976.

Mark Twain's Speeches. New York and London: Harper and Brothers Publishers, 1910.

Mark Twain: The Complete Interviews. Edited by Gary Scharnhorst. Tuscaloosa: The University of Alabama Press, 2006.

Mark Twain: Wit and Wisecracks. Edited by Doris Benardete. Mount Vernon, New York: Peter Pauper Press, 1961.

My Autobiography: "Chapters" from the North American Review. Mineola, New York: Dover, 1999. (Note that "Autobiography" (no italics, no quotes) indicates one of the many sources of his autobiography, including *Mark Twain in Eruption.*)

The Mysterious Stranger and Other Stories. Mineola, New York: Dover, 1992.

The Oxford Companion to Mark Twain. Gregg Camfield. Oxford and New York: Oxford University Press, 2003.

The Portable Mark Twain. Edited by Bernard De Voto. New York: Penguin Books, 1981.

When in Doubt, Tell the Truth: And Other Quotations from Mark Twain. Edited by Brian Collins. New York: Columbia University Press, 1996.

Who Is Mark Twain? The Mark Twain Foundation. New York: HarperCollins, 2009.

The Wit and Wisdom of Mark Twain: A Book of Quotations. General editor, Paul Negri. Mineola, New York: Dover, 1999.

For reference:

Critical Companion to Mark Twain: A Literary Reference to His Life and Work. Edited by R. Kent Rasmussen. New York: Facts on File, 2006.

Mark Twain: A Life. Ron Powers. New York: Free Press, 2006.

The Mark Twain Encyclopedia. Edited by J. R. LeMaster and James D. Wilson. New York: Garland Reference Library, 1993.

There are also several good online reference works, among them:

The University of California's Mark Twain Project (marktwainproject.org)
The University of Virginia's Electronic Text Center's "Mark Twain in His Times" by Stephen Railton (http://twain.lib.virginia.edu/index2.html)
TwainQuotes.com